# CAVAPOO BI AND CAVAPOOS

# Your Perfect Cavapoo Guide

Cavapoos, Cavapoo Puppies, Cavapoo Training, Cavapoo Size, Cavapoo Nutrition, Cavapoo Health, History, & More!

By Mark Manfield

© DYM Worldwide Publishers, 2019.

**Published by DYM Worldwide Publishers 2019.**

978-1-913154-00-4

will not be liable for, the websites being temporarily or being removed from the Internet. The accuracy and completeness of the information provided herein, and opinions stated herein are not guaranteed or warranted to produce any particular results, and the advice or strategies, contained herein may not be suitable for every individual. The author, publisher, distributors, and/or affiliates shall not be liable for any loss incurred as a consequence of the use and application, directly or indirectly of any information presented in this work. This publication is designed to provide information regarding the subject matter covered. The information included in this book has been compiled to give an overview of the topics covered. The information contained in this book has been compiled to provide an overview of the subject. It is not intended as medical advice and should not be construed as such. For a firm diagnosis of any medical conditions, you should consult a doctor or veterinarian (as related to animal health). The writer, publisher, distributors, and/or affiliates of this work are not responsible for any damages or negative consequences following any of the treatments or methods highlighted in this book.

Website links are for informational purposes only and should not be seen as a personal endorsement; the same applies to any products or services mentioned in this work. The reader should also be aware that although the web links included were correct at the time of writing they may become out of date in the future. Any pricing or currency exchange rate information was accurate at the time of writing but may become out of date in the future. The Author, Publisher, distributors, and/or affiliates assume no responsibility for pricing and currency exchange rates mentioned within this work.

# Table of Contents

# Introduction

A dog breed known for its adorable looks and sweet personality, the Cavapoo is quickly gaining in popularity worldwide. The Cavapoo is what is known as a "designer dog," a term which is used interchangeably with hybrid, cross-breed, or mixed breed. The Cavapoo carries both the Poodle and the Cavalier King Charles Spaniel in its pedigree. Most typically, the Miniature Poodle is the preferred size Poodle for breeding, resulting in puppies who will eventually weigh between 12-25 lbs (6.8kg – 11.3kg). The Cavapoo is ideally the perfect combination of the two breeds which comprise its parentage, and who are both known for their affectionate, charming natures. The breed is hallmarked by its friendly personality. A loving breed, Cavapoos bond deeply with their families and thrive in a home with children. The Cavapoo is known to be a dog breed of medium size, making them the ideal lap dog. A true mixed breed, the Cavapoo's coat comes in many different color combinations and textures.

The Cavapoo is a dog that is always up for an adventure. Wherever its family goes, this pooch will be only too happy to tag along. If there is some playtime involved, that's all the better. A dog of moderate activity requirements, a Cavapoo does not need to be worn out. A daily walk of average length will do. The

Cavapoo is a dog breed that loves to please its people, making it a pleasure to train.

Since the Cavapoo is a cross-breed, it is currently not a breed that is recognized by any kennel club. A dog who excels as a family companion, the Cavapoo's sole purpose is to love their families and bring them joy.

The Cavapoo's coat is considered by some to be hypoallergenic; however, there is no scientific proof to support this claim. Many Cavapoos, who most closely resemble the Poodle portion of their pedigree, will bear lower shedding properties than other puppies who favor the Cavalier King Charles Spaniel genes. Dogs who shed less frequently have been credited with a reduced immune response in allergy sufferers.

*The Cavapoo is a loving, affectionate dog who thrives in a family with children.*

A breed who many different countries lay claim to including the United States and Australia, this happy-go-lucky dog is known as a breed of exuberant spirit. The Cavapoo's playful, intelligent nature makes him a pleasure to live with and to train. The Cavapoo is sometimes referred to as a Cavoodle, a name which also reflects its parentage as being a cross between a Cavalier King Charles Spaniel and a Poodle. Since this breed is a cross-breed and is relatively new in its origins, there is no consistent set of traits that definitively identify the breed at present. Many love the Cavapoo for specifically this reason.

At this time, the Cavapoo does not have a lengthy breed history. However, it is believed that the Cavapoo was created out of a desire to create a loyal, happy family dog with low-shedding properties. The Cavapoo is a breed that benefits from early socialization to allow the dog to acclimate easily to new environments.

A hardy breed, the Cavapoo typically lives from 10-13 years with excellent quality of life and few health problems. Among the health conditions which can befall Cavapoos are the following: mitral valve disease (heart problems), hip dysplasia, and luxating patellas.

Cavapoos are a people-oriented breed. As such, they do not do well when left isolated for lengthy periods of time. A very intelligent breed, Cavapoos benefit from regular mental and physical stimulation to satisfy their desire for exercise and to use their brain.

Because of their friendly nature, the Cavapoo makes a poor guard dog. The Cavapoo is highly sociable and will happily greet a stranger as a long-lost friend, an endearing quality. Though the Cavapoo must learn manners as with all dog breeds, it is quick to learn and not given to rude behavior by nature. When it comes to cuteness, it's hard to beat the Cavapoo. This breed's charming personality and stunning good looks make it a favorite of many families worldwide. If you add one to your brood, you'll find they are just like potato chips. It's hard to stop at just one!

# CHAPTER 1

# Cavapoo History and Origins: Where Did They Come From?

Since the Cavapoo is a breed of recent origins, there is not yet a comprehensive written history for this adorable pooch. Today, we learn much of what we know about this popular dog breed from its genetic descendants. The Cavapoo is a cross-breed dog, meaning the breed was developed by mating two dogs of different purebred dog breeds to create the new hybrid we know of as the Cavapoo. Several different countries lay claim to the origins of the Cavapoo, including the United States and Australia. In truth, it is likely that both countries were experimenting with creating this cross-breed at the same time, and both deserve some credit when it comes to the breed's origins. The Cavapoo is a happy little fellow. A lover of children, this dog is well-suited to family living. Not a breed of extremes, this happy-go-lucky canine needs only a moderate amount of exercise; but to remain truly content, the Cavapoo requires lots of quality time with its family. An easy-going pooch, the Cavapoo adapts well to new environments, making this dog a joy to take anywhere. Though history is still being written for this beloved designer dog breed, one thing is certain: the Cavapoo is here to stay, and we are glad of it.

*The Cavapoo is a cross-breed which takes half of its pedigree from the Poodle, whether Standard (pictured above), Miniature, or Toy.*

The Cavapoo, a dog breed alternately known as the Cavoodle, takes its name from its two purebred parents: the Cavalier King Charles Spaniel and the Poodle, whether Standard, Miniature, or Toy-sized. This cross-breed was undertaken with a specific purpose. The original breeders of this hybrid sought to create a dog that would remain small in size, and that was characterized by a personality that was upbeat and friendly. In addition to this, a coat with low shedding properties that would be unlikely to induce allergic reactions in family members and friends was also highly desirable.

## What is a Cavapoo?

The Cavapoo is considered to be a designer dog. This term is also used interchangeably with cross-breed, hybrid, and mixed breed. To create a designer dog, a breeder combines two dogs of different purebred types to produce an entirely new breed. The hope is to create a dog which is the ideal mix of the positive traits of both parents and their respective breeds. The Cavapoo's pedigree is comprised of the breeding of a Cavalier King Charles Spaniel with a Poodle. Since the Cavapoo is a dog of mixed breed origins, it needed a name which would be an accurate representation of its true heritage. With this in mind, the two purebred breed names were combined to produce a name worthy of this adorable new hybrid. This exciting new designer dog is known as the Cavapoo, or by some, as the Cavoodle. Though we cannot trace the Cavapoo's origins to a specific date, we do know that the breed enjoyed an immense surge of popularity in the United States in the 1990s and remains a staple in the homes of families worldwide today.

The Cavapoo is not a dog breed with an extensive history. However, both of the Cavapoo's parents, the Cavalier King Charles Spaniel and the Poodle, are breeds with long, well-recorded pasts. The Cavalier King Charles Spaniel, a member of the toy grouping of breeds as designated by kennel clubs, is a dog who enjoys a heritage tracing back to the Renaissance era. The Cavapoo takes its size and sweet, friendly nature from the people-loving, affectionate Cavalier King Charles Spaniel portion of its pedigree. The Cavalier King Charles Spaniel is well-renowned for its even-temperedness. The breed's naturally calm demeanor makes this dog well-suited to family living and an excellent companion for children. A breed known for its easy adaptability to new circumstances, the Cavalier King Charles Spaniel, is not afraid of new experiences and approaches new people and animals with enthusiasm and confidence. A dog with connections to 17th-century royalty, there is a regal air about this charming breed whose sweet expression easily melts even the hardest of hearts.

The Cavalier King Charles Spaniel of old looked markedly different from the dog we know of today. In the 17th century, King Charles the I and his son Charles the II formed deep attachments to a black and tan spaniel breed known as the Toy Spaniel. The breed remained vastly popular with members of the nobility up until the 19th century. During the reign of Queen Victoria, the Toy Spaniel was bred to dogs of Asian descent, such as Japanese Chins and Pugs, to create a new breed known as the English Toy Spaniel. However, the English Toy Spaniel possessed a dome-shaped head and a face that was flatter in dimension and brought along with it some breathing challenges. During this time, the original Toy Spaniel so beloved by King Charles the I and Charles the II nearly became extinct. However, many remembered the Toy Spaniels of old and longed for a return to the breed which graced many artist renderings and paintings from the 17th century. With this in mind, an American benefactor named Roswell Eldridge issued a challenge to English breeders in the 1920s. If one could produce a dog that more closely resembled the Toy Spaniels of King Charles the I and Charles the II's day, he would award them with a generous cash prize. The dog he sought was referred to as "Blenheim Spaniels of the Old World type," a reference to a breed of red and white spaniels who made their home at the Blenheim Palace during the early

19th century. The cash prize was enough to set these 1920's British breeders to work to recreate the almost forgotten breed of old. The resulting dog was dubbed the Cavalier King Charles Spaniel. The name King Charles was taken from the dog's roots as the beloved black and tan spaniel of King Charles the I and Charles the II's day. Cavalier was a nod to the ruling party at the time who threw their support behind the Stuart family that ultimately beheaded Charles the I. A slightly macabre name for a much-loved and adorable dog breed, but one that pays homage to its true history.

The Standard Poodle traces its origins to Germany, where its primary purpose was hunting ducks. The Standard Poodle is considered the national dog of France. Since the Poodle was originally bred to retrieve ducks from water, it is most certainly a water-loving breed, a trait that may or may not be passed down to its Cavapoo offspring. The Poodle is a breed with a history that spans more than 400 years. Since the Poodle's coat is typically very low shedding, it makes this breed the ideal mate for the Cavalier King Charles Spaniel if the desired outcome was to create a dog of small size, sweet nature, and a low to no-shedding coat. The Poodle is a breed of exceptional intelligence, a trait this dog passes on to its Cavapoo children. The Poodle is elegant in appearance and regal in stature. From the brush, hunting by the side of its owner to the salons of the rich and famous, the Poodle takes pride of place by the sides of diverse and varied people worldwide. In addition to its natural retrieving ability and innate intelligence, the Poodle has a strong sense of smell, making the breed the ideal companion for tracking work, scent detection or even sniffing out luxurious truffles in the woods.

The combination of these two breeds was really quite ingenious. The goal was to create a dog requiring minimal maintenance, which remained small of size, and with a friendly, outgoing personality. The pairing was highly successful in creating the popular and deeply loved breed we know of today as the Cavapoo.

*The Cavalier King Charles Spaniel (pictured above) is the other purebred breed which makes up the Cavapoo's pedigree. The coat color in the dog in the picture is known as Blenheim (chestnut-colored markings on a white background).*

## Where Did the Cavapoo Come From?

The Cavapoo's true origins are unknown. It is believed that this dog pairing was first attempted in the mid-1980s in either Australia or the United States, or possibly even both. The breed has gained immense popularity over the years with a true interest in the breed beginning in the 1990s. It is most likely that the interest in this particular hybrid was spurred by the popularity of the Goldendoodle, a mixed breed achieved by mating a Golden Retriever to a Poodle. Many different hybrids have been created since that time, with the Cavapoo being yet another of them. The intent of most of the breeders of these mixed breed dogs was partially to create a dog breed that would be amenable to life with a family of allergy sufferers. The one common denominator between many of these cross breeds is the inclusion of the Poodle as one of the dogs in the breeding pair. This, of course, is due to the Poodle's coat having low to no-shedding properties, thus reducing the potential for allergic reactions to shed dander via hair in the family's home environment.

## What Was the Original Purpose of the Cavapoo?

The Cavapoo was bred for one purpose and one alone...to be a true family dog in every sense of the term. In this goal, breeders of the Cavapoo were highly successful. The Cavapoo remains a loyal, loving family companion. A dog that thrives in the company of its "people," the Cavapoo is easy to train, bonds deeply to its family, and is known for its happy-go-lucky ways.

The Cavapoo is a breed that enjoys engaging in activities with its family. An easily trainable breed that loves to please, the Cavapoo is eager to learn new skills.

## Is the Cavapoo an Old Breed?

The exact age of the Cavapoo is unknown; however, best estimates date the breed as originating in the mid-1980s. Armed with this information, we can conclude that the Cavapoo is not an old breed. However, this breed has become tremendously popular, ensuring that though its history is not currently long, the Cavapoo is one dog that is here to stay.

## How is the Cavapoo Different from the Cavachon, Cockapoo, or Havapoo?

Though many of the names sound similar, there are differences between the Cavapoo, the Cavachon, the Cockapoo, and the Havapoo. The main difference between each of these cross breeds is found in the dogs which comprise their pedigrees. The Cavapoo is created by mating a Cavalier King Charles Spaniel to a Poodle. The Cavachon retains the Cavalier King Charles Spaniel portion of the Cavapoo's pedigree, but instead of the Poodle as the second parent in the pairing, the dog is mated to a Bichon Frise. The Cockapoo retains the Poodle portion of the Cavapoo's pedigree but replaces the Cavalier King Charles Spaniel with a Cocker Spaniel. And lastly, the Havapoo combines a Havanese with a Poodle. As with other newly generated cross-breeds, it is not recommended at this time that a Cavapoo be bred directly to another Cavapoo. The breed is too new in its inception for the novice breeder to combine two hybrids in a breeding pair without risking grave health problems in the resulting puppies. At this time, it is recommended that Cavapoo puppies be produced by reputable breeders who carefully select health tested, genetically and temperamentally stable dogs with one of each breed represented: a Cavalier King Charles Spaniel to a Poodle. In time, there will be sufficient genetic diversity within the pool of available breeding dogs that a Cavapoo can safely be bred to another Cavapoo. But as with all good things, this will take time to achieve.

## The Cavapoo vs. the Cockapoo

The Cavapoo and the Cockapoo bear more similarities than they do differences. The main thing that sets them apart from each other is their parentage. While the Cavapoo is created by breeding a Cavalier King Charles Spaniel to a Poodle, the Cockapoo maintains the Poodle portion and replaces the Cavalier King Charles Spaniel with a different spaniel entirely: the Cocker.

Though both breeds have similar coat types and textures and enjoy personality traits that are much the same, there are two main differences between the two breeds. The Cockapoo typically enjoys a longer life expectancy. The average lifespan of a Cavapoo is from 13-15 years with the Cockapoo topping out at 14-18 years by comparison.

The other significant difference deals with how each of the breeds responds to the absence of their families. Though both breeds bond very deeply with their people, the Cavapoo is quite content to remain at home for short periods of time while its owner is away. The Cockapoo is more prone to experiencing bouts of separation anxiety and is not well-suited to spending much time alone.

## The Cavapoo vs. the Maltipoo

The Maltipoo differs from the Cavapoo in that it is a combination of a purebred Maltese to a purebred Poodle. The Maltipoo shares its naturally cheerful nature in common with the Cavapoo. They are well known to be a very friendly breed that is hallmarked by its sunny personality; all traits the Maltipoo shares in common with the Cavapoo.

One of the main differences between the Maltipoo and the Cavapoo is coat color. The Maltipoo typically comes in shades of white, cream, and silver, whereas the sky is the limit when it comes to color variations for the Cavapoo.

The other area of significance is the amount of vocalization you can expect from either of these breeds. The Cavapoo is generally a quiet dog who is not known to bark much. However, the Maltipoo loves to express itself vocally and is known to be quite a barker. This trait is most likely derived from the Maltese portion of its pedigree.

## The Cavachon vs. the Cavapoo

The Cavachon differs from the Cavapoo in that it drops the Poodle portion of the pedigree in favor of the amiable Bichon Frise. The Cavachon is available in two size variations: the Small and the Toy Cavachon. The small Cavachon more closely resembles the size of the Cavapoo with weights ranging from 15 to 20 or more lbs. The Toy Cavachon is much smaller by comparison and weighs between 10 to 14 lbs. The Cavapoo's average weight is typically as low as 12 to as high as 25 lbs as an average.

By nature, the Cavachon tends to be a more laid back pooch than its more exuberant Cavapoo counterpart.

Beyond these few differences, the two breeds are remarkably similar with both being joyful, easy-going pets that are a pleasure to live with and to train.

# CHAPTER 2

# Cavapoo Dogs— What Do You Need to Know?

N o book about Cavapoos would be complete without a chapter devoted to the unique personality traits, appearance, and behavioral characteristics of this popular breed. Purebred breeds possess a written standard which defines what the ideal dog of that breed type should look and act like. Since the Cavapoo is a cross-breed, meaning it is comprised of two different purebred breeds, and it is also so new in its inception; there is little consistency in the appearance or specific traits of this pooch. Contributing to the problem is the fact that the Poodle is available in three different size varieties, meaning that the Cavapoo can come in a wide range of sizes. By comparison, most purebred dog breeds have enjoyed hundreds of years of selective breeding, which has refined their appearance, personality traits, and working ability to a set of predictable expectations. While there can be some moving away from the ideal look and type of a purebred, this is generally the exception and not the norm.

With even the Cavapoo's size, height, and weight lacking consistency, it is easy to see how at this time, it is not possible to write a standard for this new breed. Why is that? The genetics behind the Cavapoo are spread across two different breeds with many dissimilar qualities. When combining a Cavalier King Charles Spaniel with a Poodle, any number of different qualities may rise to the surface. Add to the mix the fact that since genetics is a random game, even littermates may differ dramatically from one another. This is particularly notable when it comes to appearance. Though the ideal hope is to produce puppies who are the perfect mix of the two breeds that comprise its parentage, it is equally possible that the puppies could end up with all of the undesirable traits. Alternatively, the Cavapoo's genetics may align in such a way that the pup more closely resembles one side of its pedigree almost entirely. This is also true of breeding two purebred dogs of the same breed together; however, decades and sometimes even centuries of highly selective breeding ensure that purebred breeds will retain the same basic appearance and personality traits. Of course, some variation from the prescribed breed standard is possible in purebreds as well. However, since purebred breeds have been bred using highly selective processes throughout the years, their genetics favor the production of puppies that conform to the breed's very specific guidelines for appearance and personality traits. While some deviation may occur within purebred breeds, the resulting offspring essentially remain easily recognizable as the breed they are intended to represent and who they genetically are.

*Cavapoos may be the perfect combination of their Cavalier King Charles Spaniel x Poodle parents or favor one parent more than another.*

If you're on the fence trying to decide between several different hybrid breeds, this book will give you all of the information you need to determine if the Cavapoo is the dog for you. Life with a Cavapoo is lots of fun, but it is always good to understand upfront what you can expect from your new canine companion, and if this dog breed is a good fit for your lifestyle.

## Is a Cavapoo Right for Me?

Since the Cavapoo was specifically bred to be a low maintenance breed, they require little special effort to maintain. With only moderate activity needs, a daily walk of average length is sufficient to meet the exercise requirements of your new pooch.

The Cavapoo is a dog breed who places only low demands on its owners. Known to possess polite manners (with appropriate training), the Cavapoo is a dog breed that is simply content to be wherever its family is and doing whatever they are doing. Equally content on a walk through the woods, playing with canine pals, or snuggled up on the couch, the Cavapoo adapts easily and well to nearly every circumstance. A breed earmarked by its naturally cheerful, laid back demeanor, the Cavapoo still benefits from regular mental stimulation through training and brain games such as puzzle toys and treat balls.

The Cavapoo's easy nature makes this pooch a good fit for nearly any home, regardless of lifestyle. The only type of home a Cavapoo would not thrive in is one where the family is away for lengthy periods of time, as this is one dog breed that thrives when in the company of its people.

The one area that gives some families pause for concern when considering the Cavapoo is its grooming requirements. The Cavapoo, as with most coated dog breeds, will require regular grooming. While visiting a groomer several times a year will help keep the Cavapoo's coat looking good, families will still need to commit to a regular regime of brushing to keep this dog's coat mat and tangle-free. Some Cavapoos will more closely resemble the Poodle portion of their heritage and will require less frequent brushing than that of the dogs who bear coats more similar to the Cavalier King Charles Spaniel. Though the Cavapoo's coat is not known to be prone to picking up odors or getting excessively dirty, it will still be necessary to bathe this dog from time to time. Bathing helps to eliminate unpleasant smells, dirt, and debris from the coat and carries the added bonus of keeping the things dogs pick up in their coats when outdoors from being deposited throughout the house. As an alternative to frequent brushing at home, you could shave the Cavapoo's coat to make it easier to maintain at home. However, your dog will still need to visit a groomer several times a year to keep the clipped coat nice and short. Still, by comparison with other cross-breeds, the Cavapoo's coat is not labor-intensive to maintain.

## Are Cavapoos Good Family Dogs?

Cavapoos make wonderful family companions. A breed that is naturally happy-go-lucky, Cavapoos crave the company of people. Known for their loving, affectionate natures, Cavapoos enjoy the company of children and are gentle and tolerant with them. Teaching the Cavapoo proper canine manners early on will help this dog to understand the boundaries within its household. Cavapoos are polite and well-mannered, but as with any dog breed, must be taught what is expected of them. Though the Cavapoo is not the type to wander, it is still a good idea to provide a fenced yard for the dog to explore. A fenced space ensures your dog remains safely contained on your property and has an appropriate place for play and other activities. The Cavapoo does still need to be walked daily to truly thrive. The costs associated with keeping this breed healthy and happy are no more expensive than any dog of this size and type; however, it is important for every family to be certain that they have the financial means to care for the Cavapoo's needs through the entirety of the 13-15 years this breed can live.

**The Cavapoo is the dog for you if you are looking for one that …**

- Is of a medium build
- Has moderate grooming requirements
- Is laid back, loving, and friendly
- Is known for being well-mannered and polite
- Requires moderate daily activity

**The Cavapoo may not be the best choice for you if…**

- You spend a lot of time away from home.
- You do not want to commit to a daily walk.
- You are not interested in teaching your dog proper house manners.
- You are not prepared to brush your dog regularly and to take it for regular grooming appointments.

## What Does a Cavapoo Look Like?

Since the Cavapoo is a cross-breed, its appearance will vary depending on the genetics of the parents behind it as well as the specific traits the dog itself received from the unique dogs which form its parentage. Typically, the breed retains the soulful eyes of the Cavalier King Charles Spaniel. Its coat can vary from silky Spaniel locks to the more tight curls of the Poodle.

The consistent traits each Cavapoo should manifest are a sweet expression and a compact body of great sturdiness. The Cavapoo may come in solid colors but is also predisposed to different color patterns and markings.

*Cavapoos come in many different colors and coat types.*

## Common Cavapoo Coat Types

As a hybrid breed, the Cavapoo coat will differ dramatically depending upon the coat type of each of the parents and the dogs within those specific bloodlines. One certainty is that the ideal coat type will combine the low-shedding qualities of the Poodle and its wavy coat type with the silky tresses of the Cavalier King Charles Spaniel. The correct Cavapoo coat should be silky and somewhat wavy. The breed tends towards a coat of medium length that requires regular grooming to remain healthy and mat and tangle-free.

### The Cavapoo Puppy Coat

The Cavapoo's coat goes through a puppy stage before reaching its full adult state. During this time, the coat is quite flat and is of even length throughout the body. This type of coat is what the Cavapoo is born with and remains with the pups for the first few weeks of life. As the puppy moves into the next phase of puppy development, the coat begins to grow into either a curly coat, which is more representative of the Poodle or a hair with a wave to it.

Mid-way during the first year of life, the true coat type of the Cavapoo puppy will be seen. Some pups end up with a coat full of tight curls while others may display a coat of silky texture which contains natural waves. Regardless of whether the coat is curly or wavy, the Cavapoo's coat generally remains of medium length.

## The Cavapoo Adult Coat

Once it is determined what coat type the Cavapoo puppy will have as an adult, hair growth patterns begin to emerge. This breed develops what is known as "feathering." Feathering is essentially hair growth along the ears, legs, chest, feet, and tail. It is these sections of the Cavapoo that can become matted or tangled, and that require frequent brushing or for the hair to be trimmed to prevent knots. Feathering often appears later in life; sometimes not until the dog is one or two years of age.

## Common Cavapoo Colors Derived From Parent Breeds

### The "Accepted" Colors for Cavalier King Charles Spaniels

The Cavalier King Charles Spaniel is an AKC recognized and registered breed. There are four acceptable colors for the Cavalier King Charles Spaniel according to the AKC breed standard. Though other colors may surface at some point, they would be considered a deviation from the accepted standard and would necessitate a disqualification from the show ring. The four colors that are accepted for the Cavalier King Charles Spaniel are as follows:

- **Blenheim** – Blenheim is defined as deep chestnut-colored markings displayed on a background of white. The Blenheim should have chestnut-colored ears with color well-spaced on the head and with a white "blaze" between the eyes and ears. At the top of the skull, there may be a chestnut marking which is commonly known as the "lozenge" or the "Blenheim spot."
- **Tricolor** -The tricolor Cavalier King Charles Spaniel bears markings which are jet black and chestnut on a white background.
- **Ruby** – A dog that is completely red. The color should be deep and rich.
- **Black and Tan** – Tan markings on a background that is jet black.

## The "Accepted" Colors for Poodles

The AKC recognizes a large number of colors for Standard, Miniature, and Toy Poodles. In addition to accepted colors and color combinations, there are also preferred color markings. Here is a list of the colors and color markings accepted for Poodles by the American Kennel Club:

- Apricot
- Black
- Blue
- Brown

- Café Au Lait (a shade of brown which poses slight fading properties)
- Cream
- Grey
- Red
- Silver
- Silver Beige
- White
- Black and Apricot
- Black and Brown
- Black and Cream
- Black and Grey
- Black and Red
- Black and Silver
- Black and Tan
- Black and White
- Blue and White
- Brown and Apricot
- Brown and White
- Cream and White
- Grey and White
- Red and Apricot
- Red and White
- White and Apricot
- White and Silver

Acceptable markings include:

- Black mask
- Black markings
- White markings
- White mask

Parti-colored Poodles, or Poodles with a coat that is white at its base with patches of any other color, are disqualified from showing.

With all of this information to consider, what color can the Cavapoo be? Color genetics are determined by the bloodlines directly behind the breeding pair. The study of color genetics is complex involving a certain number of colors which express dominant genes over others. This means that certain color genes are more likely to be brought forward in any breed coupling's offspring. It is interesting to note that since the genes of many generations linger in the DNA of the breeding pair, it is possible that puppies within a Cavapoo litter may be born with colors and color combinations that the parents themselves do not have.

It is plain to see from a cursory view of the many possible colors and color combinations for each of these two breeds that there is a vast number of potential color options possible for a Cavapoo puppy.

Cavapoos can be solid-colored or can be what is considered parti-colored, with one color forming a background on which other colors are displayed.

## Cavapoo Personality Traits—What is the Cavapoo Temperament Like?

The child of two purebred breeds who have as many similarities as they do differences, the Cavapoo is intended to be the ideal blend of the Cavalier King Charles Spaniel and the Poodle's temperaments. Cavapoos are a breed of medium energy who require only a moderate amount of exercise to remain content and healthy. However, the Cavapoo is also a dog who enjoys an adventure. Whatever you've got planned for the day, your Cavapoo will happily trot along by your side and will greet each new opportunity with enthusiasm and joy!

The Cavapoo is a friendly loving breed. They are curious by nature and happily make friends of the canine and human sort, wherever they go.  A dog breed known to love and enjoy the company of children, the Cavapoo is gentle and affectionate towards kids. This adorable little pooch is truly a people dog and is happiest in the company of the people it calls its family. However, the Cavapoo is a dog breed that does not do well when kept isolated from its family members for any length of time. If you are away from home for lengthy periods of time, the Cavapoo may not be the right dog for you.

As a nod to the Poodle portion of its pedigree, the Cavapoo is a highly intelligent dog. You will find this pooch loves to train and picks up commands with ease. The Cavapoo easily has the intellect and the sturdy body composition to excel at a number of competitive dog performance sports, including agility, flyball, Rally-O, and obedience.

The Cavapoo is not a breed known for an intense prey drive. However, it is good to bear in mind that Spaniels were often used in hunting and retrieving work, and the Poodle's original purpose was to work alongside its owner in duck hunting. With this in mind, your Cavapoo may have the drive to work which can be productively channeled into many different activities including games of fetch, tug, or doing some trick training. It will also be important to provide some form of secure containment system within your backyard to keep your Cavapoo safe on your property.

Though the Cavapoo is a gentle-natured breed that bonds closely to people, they are not especially sensitive. Still, this dog breed should be treated with care during training exercises. The Cavapoo is an eager participant in learning sessions and is not known to be stubborn. A breed of above-average intelligence, you will want to be sure your Cavapoo not only gets regular physical exercise but that you also provide some brain games to keep your pooch's mind active and engaged.

Providing regular daily exercise and sufficient mental stimulation will help your Cavapoo remain the laid back, happy-go-lucky pup it was intended to be. You will find your Cavapoo pup will actively seek your company and is content resting by your side on the couch or off in search of adventure. A breed that adapts easily to nearly every circumstance, the Cavapoo has the spirit of an explorer and the willingness to try anything with its favorite person by its side.

A naturally polite dog, your Cavapoo will be a delight to be around. This natural inclination, however, cannot take the place of proper manners training. The effort you expend to teach your

Cavapoo appropriate canine manners will yield great rewards. The breed is well known as a true gentleman. But all dogs benefit from being taught boundaries, and the Cavapoo most definitely will need to receive this training from you as well.

The one consistent trait you will find amongst Cavapoos is their gentle, loving nature. A breed known to display lots of affection and to thrive when in close contact with its people, it is hard not to fall in love with the Cavapoo!

## Cavapoo Breed Characteristics—What Behavior Can You Expect from Your Cavapoo?

The Cavapoo truly is a mild-mannered dog. You will find this breed is not given to any excesses with the exception of its penchant for lavishing its favorite people with kisses.

If you add a Cavapoo to your family, you will be delighted to discover that you now share your home with a pooch that is respectful, polite, and exceptionally well-mannered; all traits that will make you the envy of any dog owner!

The Cavapoo loves to please its people, making it an easy breed to train. With the intelligence to back up its eagerness, the Cavapoo picks up commands with ease.

## What Jobs Can the Cavapoo Do?

Though the Cavapoo is not a working dog, it certainly possesses the heritage to assist its owner on a hunt. Since both the Cavalier King Charles Spaniel and the Poodle possess excellent scent detection capabilities and are natural retrievers, the Cavapoo has the potential to excel in either of these arenas.

But the most common role of the Cavapoo is simply to be a loyal, loving companion to its family, a job which this breed has truly mastered.

## Can a Cavapoo Be a Show Dog?

At this time, the Cavapoo is still inconsistent in appearance and breed traits, and as such, it lacks a written standard. In time, as selective breeding yields a more consistent breed type; pioneers in the breed will write one and move through the appropriate channels to seek official breed recognition. Until this is accomplished, Cavapoos are not eligible to compete in conformation events.

In recent years, both the AKC and the Canadian Kennel Club have moved to allow cross-breeds to participate in performance sports events alongside purebred registered dogs. This allows the Cavapoo and other hybrid dog breeds to enter and obtain titles in such events as agility, Rally-O, obedience, lure coursing, and scent detection.

## Can Cavapoos Be Left Alone?

While Cavapoos can be successfully left alone, they are a breed that craves the company of people. You will not find your Cavapoo will be destructive during your absence; however, you will want to limit the amount of time your pooch spends isolated from you since the breed does best when surrounded by its loved ones.

## Do Cavapoos Get Along with Other Animals?

This happy-go-lucky breed loves the company of other animals! An unassuming, gentle soul, the Cavapoo is unlikely to be offensive to other dogs. Quite the opposite! This dog breed's friendly nature invites other dogs to come to enjoy some playtime with your pooch.

However, all dogs, regardless of breed, should be properly introduced to other canines. To do this, it is important to begin the socialization process as early as possible. Always take care to only expose your Cavapoo to dogs who are trusted, socially appropriate, and well-mannered.

Cavapoos can easily live in a household with cats. Since they lack an intense prey drive, they are also well-suited to life with animals such as rabbits, guinea pigs, or hamsters.

## Are Cavapoos Good with Children?

Cavapoos have one favorite thing in life: people! And if a Cavapoo had to pick its favorite person, it just might pick a child. Cavapoos are exceptionally well-suited to families with children. They are gentle and tolerant. Their affectionate nature makes them the ideal companion for kids.

As with any dog breed, you should carefully observe all interactions between your Cavapoo and children. Though an exceptionally patient breed, accidents can easily happen, and even the most gentle-natured and tolerant dog can become annoyed by what it perceives as rough treatment or annoying behavior. It is your responsibility to protect both your dog and your child, and the best way to do that is to actively supervise all playtime.

## Cavapoo Puppy Names

When it comes time to choosing a name for your new Cavapoo puppy, you are sure to have a ball!

Here is a list of some of the most popular puppy names for boys:

- Ace
- Apollo
- Benny
- Benji
- Bear
- Frankie
- Gizmo
- Gunner
- Rufus
- Simba
- Toby
- Jax

Here is a list of popular puppy names for girls:

- Stella
- Chloe
- Coco
- Nala
- Sadie
- Senna
- Willow
- Lola
- Trixie
- Mocha
- Luna
- Dixie

# CHAPTER 3

# Cavapoo Types

I f you think the Cavapoo is the dog for you, the next decision you will have to make is what size dog you'd like to add to your family. Think a Mini Cavapoo is the dog for you? Or maybe a Standard is your ideal fit!

## Miniature Cavapoos or the Mini Cavapoo

Most often achieved by breeding a Cavalier King Charles Spaniel to a Miniature Poodle, the Miniature Cavapoo is the perfect addition to any home. Purchasing a Miniature Cavapoo gives you all of the great traits of the Standard but in a smaller package. The Miniature Cavapoo is smaller in height than its Standard counterpart, measuring between 9" (22.86cm) -14" (35.56cm) at the withers (highest point of the shoulder). When it comes to weight, the Miniature Cavapoo ranges from 7 to 18 lbs (3-8 kg). The Mini Cavapoos at the smaller end of the size and weight spectrum are ones whose parentage most often consists of a Cavalier King Charles Spaniel bred to a Toy Poodle, instead of a Miniature.

## Standard Cavapoos

Following along the same path, the breeding of a Cavalier King Charles Spaniel to a Standard Poodle will result in what is known as Standard Cavapoo offspring. The Standard Cavapoo falls within the same height range as the Miniature but is more likely to favor the higher end of the spectrum with 12" (30.48cm) -14" (35.56cm) at the withers being the average. Weight-wise, the Standard Cavapoo is more dense at 12-25 lbs (5-11 kg). The Standard Cavapoo is considered a dog of moderate sturdy build, and this size variation is the most popular and the one most commonly associated with the breed.

## Teacup Cavapoos

Though the Cavalier King Charles Spaniel is considered a toy breed by the AKC and other kennel clubs, it is not "toy" in size. The Poodle is available in three different size variations: the Standard, Miniature, and Toy. Since neither of these breeds is available in Teacup varieties, neither is the offspring of this mated pair. Should you encounter a breeder offering Teacup Cavapoos, beware. The Cavapoo is not available in Teacup sizing and cannot safely be produced in this size variant.

## Are Cavapoos a Recognized Breed?

Currently, the Cavapoo is not a recognized breed. It is possible that with more consistent breed traits produced through selective breeding over a longer period of time that a breed standard will be finalized and accepted by an official kennel club. Though the Cavapoo is not eligible for registration with the AKC, the Canadian Kennel Club, or any other registration body of such nature, the breed can be registered with several different agencies which provide registration services for cross-breeds as well as pedigree tracking software.

# What are Some Common Cavapoo Characteristics?

The Cavapoo has some characteristics that are quite common to the breed. Though not high energy by definition, this is one breed that can keep up with whatever adventure you've got in mind.

The Cavapoo's temperament leans towards a genial pet who is good-natured, gentle, and extremely friendly. A happy breed, the Cavapoo is not only easy to please, but it is also a pooch that lives to delight its people.

Cavapoos are most happy when in the company of its beloved family. Easily adaptable to new circumstances and opportunities, this pooch is a joy to take anywhere.

## What is the Average Cavapoo Weight?

Because the Cavapoo is available in both Standard and Miniature sizes and is of mixed breed origins, it is difficult to give a precise weight you can expect from your Cavapoo. However, on average, a fully grown Cavapoo will weigh between 12-25 lbs (5-11 kg)

## What is the Average Adult Cavapoo Size?

As with assessing the average Cavapoo adult weight, it is a challenge to give an accurate reflection of what size you can expect your dog to be when fully grown. As an approximation, an adult Cavapoo will range between 9"-14" (23-25 cm) in height at the withers.

# CHAPTER 4

# Cavapoo Breeders and Buying a Cavapoo—How Can You Find a Quality Cavapoo?

So, you are ready to add a Cavapoo puppy to your family! Your first step is finding a reputable breeder from which to obtain your new canine bundle of joy. Today, the internet has made it easier for people to list and sell puppies for sale across the globe. While this convenience makes it easier to source a puppy of any breed at any time, it is far more challenging to find a Cavapoo puppy produced and supported by a responsible, committed breeder. After all, you don't want to buy just any puppy. You want to set yourself up for success by taking all of the necessary measures to try to purchase a puppy that is the most likely to enjoy good health, and that has been bred from parents of sound temperament and conformation.

To date, the breeding of cross-breeds is not governed by any regulating body. This means that any individual who happens to possess both a Cavalier King Charles Spaniel and a Poodle has the liberty to mate them to create a litter of Cavapoo puppies.

But responsible breeding is based on more than simply putting together any two dogs for the sake of puppies to meet buyer demand. Responsible breeders are committed to the health, future, and longevity of their breed. They take the time to vigorously health test their breeding stock to ensure the absence of genetic disease. They are devoted to appropriate rearing practices and to providing early socialization for every puppy they produce. Why? Because responsible breeders take producing puppies of sound health, conformation, and temperament seriously. They recognize that the future of their beloved breed depends on it.

So, where can you look for a Cavapoo puppy from a breeder you can trust? Many families who wish to add a Cavapoo to their family start their search with the International Designer Canine Registry (IDCR)(http://designercanineregistry.com). This organization, known by the acronym IDCR, is a registry for hybrid breeds. This registry offers their services to breeders worldwide, meaning you will have easy access to the most comprehensive resource for Cavapoo breeders that is available today. IDCR offers full registration services to hybrid breeds and designer dogs. Those who choose to use their registration services also have the opportunity to track their pedigrees via the website's online pedigree software. The list of registered IDCR breeders is available to the public at no cost.

Another great option is the National Hybrid Registry (http://www.nationalhybridregistry.com) (NHR). This registration body requires that all breeders wishing to use their services provide tangible proof that the offspring were produced from two purebred parents.

UK residents have the option of using the Designer Dogs-The Kennel Club (https://www.thekennelclub.org.uk) to assist with their search for the ideal Cavapoo. DDCR seeks to unite dog seekers with dog breeders. This organization is based in the UK and offers full registration services to breeders of both purebred and hybrid dog breeds.

*You will need to find a reputable breeder from which to purchase your Cavapoo puppy.*

## Cavapoo Puppies for Sale—What to Look for When Buying a Cavapoo

Any search for a puppy begins with a list of things you should look for and warning signs to avoid. Unfortunately, popular breeds become a target for unscrupulous people whose sole goal is to mass-produce puppies to make a quick buck. Often referred to as "puppy mills" or "commercial breeders," these types of operations should be avoided at all costs. Puppy mills, in particular, are known purveyors of disease as a result of the cruel and unsanitary conditions in which they house not only puppies but also the mother of these little souls as well. Health testing of breeding stock is of no concern to these types of breeders. Sadly, they have little to no genuine concern or affection for the health and mental well-being of any of the animals in their care. They are often confined to wire cages, which are far too small to allow for even the smallest movement, torture for any living being to endure. Many sit in their own waste materials, their bodies overcome with illness, sores, and disease. Sadly, these dogs most often never receive any veterinary care. Once a dog can no longer serve its purpose as a moneymaker for the breeder, it is often euthanized or thrown out on the street to fend for itself. Most cruel of all is the fact that these precious dogs have never known true love or the affection of a loving owner. They have never had the experience of feeling their little paw pads on grass or of eating delicious, high-quality meals that have been optimized to promote their health. Most have never seen a toy or felt the comfort of a soft blanket or bed. Though life is far less than joyful for these dogs, their deaths are often even more heartbreaking. In a last-ditch effort to make money from the dogs, many are sold to medical clinics to be used in laboratory experiments. Others are simply thrown away to die alone or become someone else's problem. To buy a puppy from such an organization is to risk purchasing a puppy that could have been exposed to disease and may be the product of parents of far less than optimal health. But more than that, it perpetuates the problem of puppy mills as the more people who buy from these operations, the more they continue to produce puppies to meet what they perceive as a very lucrative demand.

Though many puppy mill puppies are sold directly off the breeder's property, many can also be found in local pet stores. Sadly, these puppies are often removed from their mothers as young as four weeks of age, a critical time in a puppy's development and socialization where the pup should be learning integral life lessons from its mother. These weeks of missed opportunity cannot be replaced by any human training. The lost opportunity leads to stunted emotional and social development in the puppies and leaves them ill-equipped to handle the challenges they will face navigating the human world in a canine body.

Online marketplaces also pose problems for the puppy buyer. Since no screening is required of those placing an ad, online marketplaces become a haven for unscrupulous breeders to offload their puppies to unsuspecting buyers. Unfortunately, many making use of this service have failed to provide even the most basic care for the dogs and puppies in their homes. If you see a Cavapoo puppy available at a bargain price, run! Puppy prices that seem too good to be true often are. All too often, the up-front bargain price for your puppy will come with expensive medical costs as the puppy grows into an adult.

Another warning sign to heed is a Cavapoo breeder who consistently has puppies available on a year-round basis. Raising a litter of puppies properly takes a lot of time, resources, and effort. Socializing a puppy to fit well into its new home is a full-time job and one that reputable breeders take very seriously. Any breeder who continuously has puppies available for sale may indeed be a commercial breeding facility which is breeding far more frequently than what it is advisable. This type of operation places the health of their breeding stock and their offspring at risk. Ethical breeders committed to safe and healthy breeding practices most often have a maximum of two to three litters per year. Typically, these types of breeders have a long list of individuals interested in adding one of their Cavapoo puppies to their home.

Pay attention to the number of times a female has been bred throughout her lifetime. For the health of the female in question, she should only be bred a few times in her youth, then should be "retired" to enjoy life as a pampered pet dog. If, in your search for a Cavapoo puppy, you run across a breeder who continually breeds her females, and particularly, if those females do not get a break between litters, you are best to continue your search elsewhere.

Often, to obtain a Cavapoo puppy from a breeder of excellent reputation, you will need to place yourself on a waiting list. Waiting lists can be as short as a few months or as long as several years. However, finding a breeder whose puppies are in great demand gives you confidence that the breeder you are considering produces puppies that others recognize as being of excellent quality. This type of puppy is most definitely worth the wait.

So, you know what to look for in identifying a reputable Cavapoo breeder. What should you look for when it comes to your Cavapoo puppy?

The first decision you will need to make regarding your Cavapoo puppy is which sex you feel is the best choice for your family. You may have strong feelings regarding your puppy gender preference, so it is important to decide ahead of time whether it is a boy or a girl you would like to add to your home. Bear in mind that a particular attachment to one gender over another may increase your time on a waiting list as certain genders may be more popular with puppy buyers. Some breeders will allow you to express which gender you prefer but will reserve the final puppy "pick" for themselves. Though many families like to have the opportunity to choose their new canine bundle of joy for themselves, there is a lot of wisdom in allowing an experienced breeder to make this selection for you. Why is that? Reputable breeders know their puppies best, and they take the time to get to know each of their puppy buyers, so they can truly understand what type of personality and activity will fit best in their homes. The breeder loves all of the puppies equally and will not be swayed by looks or individual puppy quirks. They can objectively select a puppy that has the right qualities to fit well into your home, thus setting you up for success right from Day One.

Personality will also make a big difference in the Cavapoo puppy you ultimately bring home. That's why taking the time to visit your breeder of choice to see your puppy's litter in its home environment is so important. It is never a good idea to select a puppy based on appearance, no matter how cute that particular puppy might be. Nor is it advisable to choose the crazy high energy puppy if you fancy yourself more of a couch potato. Be realistic about what you have to offer your Cavapoo puppy and allow that information to guide your selection process. Even at the tender age of six to eight weeks of age, it is possible to glimpse the personality your puppy will have as an adult.

Visiting your Cavapoo puppy's first home is always an excellent idea. While you are there, be sure to ask your breeder if you may meet your puppy's parents. Taking the time to spend time with the parents of your Cavapoo puppy will give you powerful insights into what you may be able to expect when your puppy reaches full maturity. Since the Cavapoo is a cross-breed, your puppy's parents may not exactly represent what your dog will look like when fully grown. However, you will be able to imagine what the ideal size and height would be of the offspring of the breeding pair based on what you see before you. This is also a great time to observe temperament. Always bear in mind that temperament can be shaped by a puppy's environment, but it is mostly genetic. If you don't like what you see in your puppy's parents, you will not like what you see in your adult Cavapoo puppy either. Since temperament is largely influenced by genetics, it is not difficult to see why an aggressive dog should never, EVER be bred.

Bear in mind that not all breeders own both dogs in the breeding pair. Many breeders own the  mother dog and pay a stud fee for the use of a male dog who belongs to a different kennel. The breeder of your puppy should have all of the pertinent information about the stud dog including health testing and the stud dog's pedigree. If you feel a visit to the stud dog is important, your breeder should be able to provide you with the necessary contact information to arrange a visit.

Since health testing is an important part of ensuring healthy puppies, you may want to ask your Cavapoo breeder if you can see copies of the parents' health clearances. Prior to any mating, both the Cavalier King Charles Spaniel and the Poodle should be stringently health tested for any possible genetic illness and physical ailment that can be common to both breeds. Only two fully healthy animals should ever be bred. It should be a big red flag to you if you request to see health testing, and the breeder makes excuses as to why you cannot see it or why they do not have it. Reputable breeders are proud to display the results of their dogs' health testing. In fact, most will provide you with these facts long before you ask!

When you visit your breeder's home, ask for the opportunity to see the area where your puppy was born as well as the area where the puppy spends most of its time. It is critical for you to understand where your puppy began its life and what it has experienced since birth. While raising a litter of puppies is messy, and puppies are busy, leaving their pen looking disheveled at times; the whelping area, the puppy rooms, and the breeder's home should be kept clean, neat, and well-organized. Be on the lookout for any signs of neglect.

It is vitally important that puppies not leave the breeder's home prior to eight weeks of age at an absolute minimum. Some breeders prefer to hang on to their puppies a little longer and let them go at ten weeks, and a rare few like to keep their babes around until 12 weeks of age. There is absolutely no reason a puppy should ever, EVER leave the breeder's home prior to eight weeks of age. If a breeder suggests picking up your puppy any sooner than eight weeks, run! You want to choose a breeder who has your puppy's best interests at heart. No matter how tempted you may be to bring your little canine bundle of joy home prior to eight weeks, you must resist that urge. Your puppy needs that critical time with its mother and littermates, and in the end, you will be glad you waited until the appropriate time to bring your Cavapoo puppy home.

## Important Questions to Ask Cavapoo Breeders

The most important part of choosing a puppy is making sure that you have done the appropriate research. You will want to formulate a list of questions to ask each breeder to help you in selecting the right Cavapoo puppy for your family. The right questions can save you time, heartache, and money.

If you find a breeder who has as many questions for you as you have for them, you've likely found a very good one. Reputable breeders don't mind being asked respectful questions. In fact, they welcome them! In addition to this, responsible breeders want the puppies they love and raise to go to a home where they will be cherished family members for life. They, as much as you, are looking for each puppy's perfect fit.

Reputable breeders do not sell their puppies to anyone who shows up with an interest and a fat wallet in hand. Most will expect you to answer an extremely detailed puppy questionnaire as a starting point. If you pass this elementary screening test, you will often be invited to meet the breeder and the puppies in person to proceed to a more formal interview.

With all of this in mind, it is a good idea to start formulating your list of questions now. Here is a sampling of some questions that will help you learn more about the breeder whose puppies you are considering.

- **Are the puppy's parents available for viewing?**

  It is important to meet your puppy's parents if possible. Taking the time to view your Cavapoo puppy's parents in their home environment affords you the opportunity to see the temperament and appearance you can likely expect in your puppy when it is fully grown. You will also have occasion to view important personality traits and the condition of the parents' coats as well. Bear in mind that a female dog who has weaned a litter of puppies will often blow coat, meaning she will not look her very best. However, what you are looking for is that the dogs are well-cared for.

- **How do you socialize your puppies?**

  Your puppy being exposed to new experiences in a positive manner is critical to your puppy's success as an adult dog. You will want to understand what your puppy has already been introduced to and what its response to the new stimulus was. Has your puppy met other friendly dogs? What did your puppy do when it first heard a loud noise? Does your puppy know what a cat is? Does the breeder make use of any popular early socialization programs such as Puppy Culture or Dr. Carmen Battaglia's Early Neurological Stimulation? This information will help you to understand what your puppy has experienced in the eight weeks it has spent with its breeder and mother dog.

- **Has the puppy been vaccinated and dewormed and at what age?**

  You should receive a detailed veterinary record which shows which vaccinations and dewormings your puppy has received and at what age. In addition to this, most breeders will provide a schedule which shows at which dates your puppy will need to visit your veterinarian for the next set of shots in its puppy series.

- **What food have you been feeding the puppy?**

  Since puppies' stomachs are very sensitive, it is never a good idea to switch your puppy's food right away. For best results, you will want to transition your puppy on a very gradual basis. To do this, simply mix in some of the new food with the old food at a ratio of half to half. Over time, you can gradually decrease the amount of old food until all that remains is the new food.

  Most breeders will send you home with a bag or small sample of the food your puppy is accustomed to. Always ask for recommended amounts and be sure to find out how many times per day your puppy is used to receiving a meal.

- **May I see the health clearances for each parent?**

  If you've done your homework, you will already be well prepared with the knowledge of what genetic diseases are common to the Cavalier King Charles Spaniel and the Poodle, and thus, to your Cavapoo puppy. This information will help you to have an informed discussion with your breeder and will help you to understand what you should be looking for in your new Cavapoo puppy. Hip dysplasia and patellar luxation are two common ailments experienced by Cavapoos, and you will want to ask the breeder for both hip scores from the OFA (Orthopedic Foundation for Animals) as well certification showing proof of normal patellas (knees) in each of the parent dogs. Both the hips and the patellas of both dogs should be in the Normal range. Common health problems and appropriate screening for breeding will be more thoroughly explored in other chapters.

- **Are there any known diseases in the lines of either parent?**

  Since the parent dogs may be clear of health problems which have presented themselves in earlier generations, you will want to ask the breeder if there are any known illnesses, diseases, or problems which have presented themselves in their bloodlines. It is valuable to know that the puppy's grandmother had Gr 1 patellar luxation (the lowest grade possible of slipping kneecaps) or that the great-great-grandfather suffered from a slight heart murmur. Of course, the further back a health issue is, the less likely you will see it in your puppy. However, it is always an excellent idea to get a clear picture of the total  health of the bloodlines of your new pooch.

- **Will the puppy come with a contract and a health guarantee? What is a health guarantee?**

  You will find that most breeders have a contract you are required to agree to and sign. A contract is a document that protects both you and the breeder and clearly outlines the expectations of both parties. Read the document with great care and be prepared to discuss it if there are aspects you don't understand or would like negotiated.

  In addition to a signed contract which outlines your responsibilities to the breeder and what they provide in terms of support for you, you should be offered a health guarantee. It is not possible for a breeder to promise you that your puppy will never befall any sort of illness, disease, or an unfortunate accident. However, the breeder should offer you a lifetime guarantee against any potential inherited diseases common to the breed. Some will offer limited guarantees, and still others will offer you conditional guarantees based on obligations you must honor in order for you to receive the benefit of the agreement. Failure to abide by the outlined conditions often results in the voiding of the health guarantee and/or contract.

- **At what age can the puppy go to its new home?**

  You now know precisely what answer you are looking for to this very specific question. If the breeder gives you any answer other than eight weeks or older, you better start shopping for a puppy from someone else.

- **What is your return policy?**

  When it comes to buying a puppy, everyone has high hopes. Unfortunately, life gets in the way of our very best plans, and sometimes a family cannot keep a puppy. You need to know ahead of time what the process is if you must return your puppy to the breeder.

You undoubtedly think this will never happen to you. But things like divorce, terminal illness, or the loss of a loved one can make caring for a dog untenable. Most reputable breeders stipulate in their contracts that if you cannot keep the dog, that the dog is to be returned to them. If you have chosen your breeder well, the reason will be irrelevant. They will welcome their puppy back with open arms, and often, with no questions asked. Some breeders take things a step further and will pursue litigation against anyone who attempts to rehome a dog without their knowledge or consent.

## The Average Cavapoo Cost—How Much Are Cavapoo Puppies?

Dog breeding is not a regulated activity, and as such, there is no such thing as standardized pricing for Cavapoo puppies. This means the price of your puppy may be an arbitrary number predetermined by your specific breeder. Unscrupulous breeders often price their puppies according to its demand. So if the puppy you have your heart set on is a highly desirable color, you may find the asking price is three to four times more than what you would pay for a pup from a reputable breeder. This is where asking the right questions and doing your homework can save a lot of heartache. Not to mention the additional strain on your pocketbook.

Another factor affecting price is where you happen to live. If you reside in an area of the world where Cavapoos are rather rare, you will certainly pay a higher price to obtain one.

As an average, you can expect to pay between $1,200 and $2,000 USD (900 to 1500 GBP) for a Cavapoo puppy. Bear in mind, that you will be able to find puppies at lower price points, and many at a much, much higher price. For this, we offer this caveat, beware of both extremes. A bargain-priced puppy is often as much a scam as the overpriced one.

## Buying a Cavapoo Adult—What Must You Consider?

Buying an adult dog can be a wonderful thing! However, you will need to consider different things when looking at an adult instead of a puppy. Many breeders will often "retire" an adult dog who is no longer being used in their breeding program. This is an excellent choice for a family that loves the breed, but that is not intent on having a puppy join their family. An adult Cavapoo comes with the added bonus of already being fully trained, saving you the expense and frustration of the puppy years.

Typically, you will find adult Cavapoos in rescues. Most often, the rescue Cavapoo finds itself in a shelter through no fault of its own. Sometimes, the dog will lack the manners it requires to live a happy canine life, and you will need to invest the man-hours into helping your new Cavapoo learn the boundaries and rules expected in your home. You will also need to be prepared to endure an adjustment period when the dog learns to acclimate to life in a new family. Still, these storms are most often weathered easily with a little patience, elbow grease, and a good sense of humor. The rescue Cavapoo is most definitely worth considering. Often some of the very best family pets can be found in your local shelter.

If you are thinking of adding an adult Cavapoo to your home, be sure to ask the rescue to provide you with a thorough health history of the dog, as well as a copy of all pertinent medical records. Whether you purchase your adult dog from a breeder, a shelter, or a rescue, your dog should come with this basic information to help you in making future medical decisions for your dog.

## Cavapoo Puppies for Adoption

Due to the breed's increasing popularity, it is not often that you see Cavapoo puppies up for adoption. However, if you do happen to luck out and find a little pup just waiting for a family like yours, it will still be important to take the time to ask the critical questions which can help you to understand the pup's background.

Among the things you will want to ask are the following:

- Why did the pup end up in rescue?
- Where is the puppy's mother?
- At what age was the puppy separated from its mother?
- What conditions were the puppy living in before being placed in rescue?
- Did the puppy receive any early socialization training?
- Is there any evidence that the puppy has been exposed to a disease or unsanitary living conditions?
- Have there been any traumatic experiences in the life of the puppy?
- What is the puppy's approximate date of birth?

- What veterinary care has the puppy received?
- Is there any known history of the puppy's parents?

Finding out as much information as you can about your rescue Cavapoo puppy will help you to understand what, if any, obstacles you may need to help your puppy overcome.

# CHAPTER 5

# Cavapoo Adoption — Adopting a Cavapoo Puppy or Adult Dog

G iving a rescue Cavapoo puppy or adult a second chance at a great life is a wonderful thing to do. Today, there are many wonderful dogs in shelters needing homes, and adopting a Cavapoo is a way to get the perfect dog for you and help a dog in need. A win-win for you and your new Cavapoo friend! The truth is many dogs end up in shelters, having done nothing to deserve their fate. If you feel the Cavapoo is your breed of choice, your local shelter or rescue is a great place to start the search for your Cavapoo family member!

*Rescue Cavapoos love to have fun too!*

## Understanding a Rescue Cavapoo's Past

Your rescue Cavapoo will come to you with a past. Sadly, that past will affect the way your pooch relates to the world around it. You will need to express patience in the initial few weeks and months your Cavapoo rescue spends in your home. Since it is rarely possible to understand what your dog has experienced prior to joining your family, it is best to give your dog all the time that it needs to adjust to its new normal. Always bear in mind that the behavior you see in the first few weeks is not necessarily a reflection of what you can come to expect. Once your dog feels at home and has the confidence that he is now firmly a family member, you will see your Cavapoo truly begin to blossom into the dog it was always meant to be.

## Rescue Cavapoos—Special Care

Rescue Cavapoos will require gentle handling and patient care. Your dog may come to you quite shut down and will need time and love to come out of their shell. During this period, you may notice some setbacks such as poor manners or accidents in your home. Always remember that your Cavapoo is still navigating the rules in its new environment and may not yet understand the expectations you have for it. Many accidents are simply a result of not knowing how to communicate to you that it needs to go outside to use the bathroom. All of these things will improve with time, consistent patience, and love.

Don't expect too much from your Cavapoo in these early stages. It is best to approach your new dog with a clean slate and to learn and grow together. Don't feel offended if your Cavapoo prefers the floor to its brand new, expensive bed, or isn't quite ready to curl up in your arms. Many rescue Cavapoos have had their trust in humans broken, and it's up to you to repair the hurts inflicted by the people who came before you. Your patience and love will be greatly rewarded, in due time.

## Reputable Cavapoo Rescues

At this time, there are no rescues devoted exclusively to the rehoming of the Cavapoo. However, this doesn't mean you will not be able to find a Cavapoo in need of a new home through other venues. All breed canine rescues often find themselves with every different breed under the rainbow, and periodically, one of those breeds will be a Cavapoo. If you are determined that the Cavapoo is the right dog for you, you could always leave your name with a number or different rescues or shelters and ask them to contact you should a Cavapoo become available.

You will also find that breeders are a great resource for Cavapoos in search of new homes. At present, this breed is still very new. For this reason, breeders stay in close contact with one another and often network to find homes for Cavapoos who come into rescue. To get on a list for a rescue Cavapoo puppy or adult, take the time to contact responsible breeders in your area to express an interest in being notified, if any Cavapoos cross their radar that need new homes.

The internet is also ripe with resources that can assist you in your search for a Cavapoo of your own to love. Online tools such as Petfinder allow you to search across the entire country for a pooch that meets your precise specifications, or that is located near to you.

## Finding Cavapoos for Adoption Near Me

To find a Cavapoo for adoption near you, the Internet is your best friend. A simple search will yield any Cavapoos within a specified region who are in need of rehoming. You can also check different online portals and private sellers who list adults or puppies in search of new homes. The same precautions apply to rescue Cavapoos sourced online as to puppies sold on online marketplaces and other internet sites. Be very careful when looking at advertisements for dogs available to new homes. You will still want to request a copy of all vaccinations and health records, as understanding your new dog's health history is vitally important. If at all possible, arrange to see the dog in its current living conditions. This will help you to understand any behavioral quirks or health issues you may see when you bring your new dog home.

If you have children, it will be even more important to ask the seller why the dog is being rehomed. Should the dog have a bite history, this rescue Cavapoo may not be the right dog for you. Your heart may be pure in wanting to adopt a rescue dog; however, not all families are equipped to deal with the needs of dogs who have behavioral problems or medical needs. You will need to gather as much information from the current owners as possible to help you make a wise decision for the dog and for your home.

## Giving Back—Volunteering with a Cavapoo Rescue

Currently, there are no organized Cavapoo rescues. But that doesn't mean that you can't help out! A great place to start is by volunteering your time and talents at your local shelter or all-breed rescue. This will put you in direct contact with any Cavapoos that do come into care and will allow you the opportunity to work specifically with them.

Rescues and shelters always welcome an extra set of hands. Whatever your skills, rescue workers will just be thrilled by your willingness and enthusiasm.

Don't have time, but have money to offer? Rescues are always in need of supplies. Contact your local shelter to find out what they could use and add a few extra items to your grocery cart for them the next time you do your shopping. Every little bit is a huge help.

Alternatively, why not volunteer to walk some dogs at your local shelter? With so many dogs who could benefit from some exercise, an added dog walker would be a huge help to the shelter workers and the dogs!

# CHAPTER 6

# Cavapoo Supplies— What You Will Need

O nce you have selected the Cavapoo puppy for you and you have your pick up date, it's time to do some shopping for your new canine arrival. Your pooch will need all kinds of fun things. Some items you can pick up ahead of time, while others are best reserved until your Cavapoo pup can join you on a trip to the pet store. Most often, your breeder will prepare you by providing tips and suggestions for all of the supplies you will need to have in place prior to bringing your new Cavapoo puppy home.

*Your Cavapoo will need lots of supplies to keep it healthy,
well-groomed, and strong.*

## Cavapoo Food–What is the Best Food and Where Do You Find It?

No one dog owner…or dog breeder…agrees on the best food to feed a dog. Each dog breed has different needs. One dog may thrive on a certain food while another of the same breed seems to languish on it. As a starting point, it is always wise to ask your breeder for food recommendations. Since your breeder has the most Cavapoo experience, they will be able to provide expert guidance to assist you in selecting the right food for your new pooch. As a general rule of thumb, it is always best to continue to feed your pup the food your breeder was giving to it prior to leaving their home. Since your Cavapoo pup will be undergoing a lot of changes during the transition from the breeder's home to yours, you don't want to introduce more change by adding in a portion of new food. Puppies cannot change foods cold turkey. For best results, you must take the time to transition to a food change gradually. Experts typically recommend that you begin by mixing the old food with the new food at a ratio of 1:1. Over time, you can gradually reduce the amount of old food until all that remains is the new food. Your puppy's bowel movements will serve as an excellent guide for you. If you see loose stools, vomiting, or diarrhea, you are transitioning too quickly, and you should step back a bit to allow your puppy's digestive system time to adjust. The process of transitioning foods should take approximately one week.

It is usually recommended that you continue with the food your breeder has selected in the early period of your Cavapoo puppy joining your home. However, your puppy's nutritional needs will change as it grows, and you will need to consider changing foods to accommodate your pup's needs. Experts in canine structure and anatomy agree that foods with a higher percentage of protein than 20 percent can harm the proper development of a puppy's skeletal structure. Foods enriched with added calcium can also lead to rapid bone growth. This poses problems because the bone grows more quickly than the corresponding muscle, leading to an unsupported skeletal system. To prevent this problem, limit your food choice to a kibble that contains no more than 20 percent protein which is sourced from the highest quality proteins available for dogs such as chicken, beef, lamb, whitefish, salmon, rabbit, kangaroo, venison, turkey, duck, or pork.

Since puppies are all highly individual, even littermates have different food requirements. With some breeds more apt to develop skin conditions and allergies, food choice becomes even more important as some dogs will react negatively to certain proteins. Thankfully, the Cavapoo is not a breed that is prone to skin problems or allergies.

The Cavapoo is a breed of moderate energy, so you will want to take care that the food that you select is not too heavily laden with calories, which could put excess weight on its small frame. To this end; bear in mind, that size matters. The Cavapoo is a small puppy that will mature into a dog of medium size. Small breed puppy food is likely fine during the early puppy months, but as your pooch develops, the tiny kibble pellets may pose too much of a choking hazard, and you will want to make the switch to larger sized kibble pieces. Also, bear in mind that your Cavapoo, who receives moderate exercise, does not need a high-octane food that is power-packed with added protein. This type of diet may, in fact, be far too rich for your dog's system. It is also dense with calories, which may cause your Cavapoo to gain weight.

As a general rule, you should select a puppy food for your Cavapoo to enjoy during the puppy years. Puppy formulations contain a slightly higher caloric content suitable to a puppy's needs as a growing youngster. These types of foods are also enriched with the correct vitamin and mineral ratios to support proper growth and development. Some companies do offer an "All Stages" blend, and this is also a good choice for you to feed your Cavapoo puppy should you choose to go this direction. During the puppy years, it is best to avoid lower-calorie adult food. Your puppy will be eating it soon enough!

It is important that you select the highest quality food that you can afford for your Cavapoo puppy. The caliber of the food you select will have an impact on your puppy's growth and overall condition. You want to choose a food that is of excellent quality, that is highly nutritious, and that contains proper balance for optimum health. Reading labels is your friend when it comes to finding just the right food for your pooch. Foods whose labels contain the words "by-products" are best avoided, particularly if the word is among the first ingredients on the label. When possible, choose a food that has an ingredients list that you understand. Though these foods are more expensive, they will save you money over time in reduced costs for veterinary care when your dog maintains excellent health.

Premium quality foods are more expensive for a valid reason. They contain high-quality ingredients and don't bulk up on fillers. What does this mean for your dog? It means your pooch gets the best possible nutrition for the price point that you pay. Many foods are full of chemicals that are largely added to preserve a long shelf life. These are best left on the shelf. If you are still uncertain as to which food to choose, ask your veterinarian for advice.

Where is the best place to source great food for your Cavapoo? Not at your grocery store. Most often, grocery stores contain foods best left at the very bottom of the food chain. Premium brand foods are most often sold at high-quality pet retailers as well as online. Some veterinary clinics will also stock them.

Raw diets have also increased in popularity today. Raw can be an excellent source of food for your dog; however, much care must be taken in the sourcing, preparation, and storage of ingredients to avoid food-borne illness. It is also important to balance all raw food with the correct minerals and vitamins to ensure balanced nutrition for your Cavapoo. Never attempt to formulate a raw diet on your own. You need a properly balanced recipe which is approved by your veterinarian.

When choosing a food for your pooch, there is one basic rule each owner should follow…choose the best food that you can afford. You do not have to buy the most expensive food your pet store carries. There are lots of moderately priced brands that will give you excellent nutrition for excellent value.

## Cavapoo Beds—What is the Most Comfortable Bedding for Your Cavapoo?

Every Cavapoo puppy needs a soft place to lay its head. Whether you plan to allow your new pooch on your furniture or to relegate it to its own dog bed is a decision which should be made well in advance of your puppy's arrival. Whatever you decide, remain consistent as your puppy will be easily confused if it is allowed to be up on the couch one minute and being scolded for scampering up there the next.

Your Cavapoo will ultimately grow to a dog of medium size. To avoid the need for the frequent replacement of dog beds, it is a good idea to purchase a bed which your dog can grow into as it matures. There is no question that small dog beds are adorable. They may fit your puppy perfectly now, but you need to keep in mind that your puppy is growing more and more every day! That cute little bed will soon more closely resemble a pillow when your Cavapoo reaches full maturity. To maximize your puppy supplies dollar, choose a bed that will also fit your dog when it is fully grown. Most dogs actually prefer a larger bed and will reject one that is too small for their size.

You will be spoiled for choice when it comes to bedding options for your Cavapoo. Your dog will appreciate your efforts to find just the right bed, but truth be told, most pooches will lay just about anywhere if it is soft and in the desired location. With this in mind, it isn't necessary to purchase the most expensive bed you can find as your dog will love the cheap bed as much as the one that leaves your wallet empty until your next payday.

Here is a list of some of the most popular dog bed styles you can choose from:

- **Orthopedic beds**

  Orthopedic beds are equipped with a layer of mattress, providing important support for your dog's bones and joints. This type of bed is most often the favorite choice of older dogs. However, puppies can also benefit from this particular style of bedding. Orthopedic beds are well made and can stand up to the abuse of a home with pets well.

- **Cave beds**

  Cave beds are increasing in popularity. Many dogs love the opportunity to nestle away in a covered area, perhaps as a throwback to their days living in actual caves in the wild. Cave beds are similar in appearance to a large boulder with an opening in the front where your dog can climb inside. Your dog can safely snuggle away inside the confines of this comfy little den. Cave beds are usually covered in very soft materials such as fleece or velour. Synthetic sheepskin is often used inside the bed to give your dog a comfortable layer of fabric against their skin. Cave bed covers are often removable, making them easy to clean. However, once the cover is off, it can prove a logistical nightmare getting it back on!

- **Heated beds**

  Who doesn't love a little heat applied to their aching joints? When it comes to heated beds, Cavapoos are definitely big fans. Heated beds provide relief for dogs suffering from sore muscles or arthritis. For dogs who really feel winter's chill, a heated bed is a great tool to take the edge off. Heated dog beds are most often simply donut beds with a heating pad installed inside the bed. Most have automatic shutoffs to ensure they are safe from accidental fires. The one negative to a heated bed is it must be plugged in in order to operate. This, of course, limits where you can place the bed as it must be nearby an outlet. A heated bed may not be the ideal choice for a puppy as puppies like to chew, and chewing cords is never a good thing.

- **Elevated beds**

  Elevated beds offer dogs the ultimate in luxury. This type of bed is most often constructed of a footed frame of PVC pipe. A layer of thick canvas is spread over the frame to allow the dog to lay suspended in the air. Elevated beds are comfortable and easy to keep clean. All you need is a wet cloth and some pet-safe cleaner, and you can wipe the dirt away in a matter of minutes. Elevated beds can also be taken outside and hosed off with a garden hose.

- **Donut beds**

  Many dogs find donut beds the best beds of all. Dogs naturally favor the donut position; hence, the shape of this particular bed. The donut bed is simply a round cushion which is covered in a soft fabric. Donut beds come in different sizes and are well-suited to the Cavapoo, in particular. Fortunately, this type of bed is extremely inexpensive so you can purchase one for every room if the mood strikes!

- **Bolster-style beds**

  Bolster-style beds are similar to the donut bed. It largely differs in its shape. Where the donut bed is round, the bolster bed is rectangular and contains "bolsters" along the sides and back where your pooch can lay their head.

- **Large pillow beds**

  The pillow bed is simple and very comfortable. They come in many different sizes and colors. The one downside to the pillow bed is it is often too large to fit in a washer and has a case which is not removable. Fortunately, they are inexpensive, so if yours gets too soiled, simply throw it away and buy a new one.

Some important considerations:

Cavapoo puppies are mischievous. Since most puppies like to explore the world with their mouths, you will need to take some things into consideration before rushing out to buy your pooch a new dog bed.

- **Is the bed durable enough to withstand puppy teeth?**

  No matter what bed you buy, your Cavapoo puppy WILL chew it. It's as certain as the fact that the sun WILL come up tomorrow morning. During this phase, it might be best to buy a bed that comes at a higher price point but with a more chew proof guarantee. If your Cavapoo puppy could set a world record for plush toy destruction, you may not want to spend a lot of money on the latest and greatest plush cave bed. Let your puppy's chewing habits be your guide in how much you spend and what type of bed you ultimately purchase.

- **Does the bed have a removable cover for washing?**

  During the puppy years, there will be accidents. There is no way around this. Unfortunately, since puppies frequently wet their beds when first waking up, you may find that some of the accidents are happening on your puppy's new bed. If you happen to own a washing machine that is equipped with a large drum, you are fortunate as you will be able to throw the entire bed in the washer and have it smelling good as new in a few hours' time. Most families don't have this luxury, meaning you will need to head to your local Laundromat or simply purchase new beds, a lot! Removable covers allow you to simply wash the affected area instead of the entire bed. They easily fit into an average-sized washer and clean up like a dream.

## Cavapoo Collars—How Do You Get the Right Fit?

There is no question that every Cavapoo puppy should have a collar. When selecting a collar, it is important that you get the correct fit. Too big and your puppy will slip out of its collar, potentially putting itself at risk. Too tight, and you've got a choking hazard on your hands.

So, just how do you get it right?

The best course of action for getting your Cavapoo a collar that fits properly is to take them with you to the store. The sales assistance can help you find the right fit. As a basic rule of thumb, the collar is the correct size if you can easily slip two of your fingers underneath it. More fingers than that, and it is too loose.

Though many collars do come with a list of sizes and breeds which typically would be able to wear that collar without issues, always bear in mind that this is a guideline only and is a poor substitute for trying the collar on your actual dog.

When you purchase your pup's first collar, remember that is just the first one of many you will purchase throughout the dog's lifetime. Your dog will grow, and as your dog grows, it will require a new collar. With this in mind, you might want to select a more budget-friendly collar for your Cavapoo's very first one. This most often means saying, "Later, leather,. We're going with nylon!" Nylon collars are available in lots of attractive colors and prints and are quite fun as they allow you to customize your choice to fit with your dog's unique personality.

## Cavapoo Leashes—How Do You Choose a Style and Length?

The length of the leash you select for your Cavapoo is dependent upon two factors: your dog's age and what your plans are for the leash. Puppies are typically best confined to a lead of no more than six feet in length. If your plans include obedience training, a six-foot lead made of leather or nylon is an excellent choice. Whether you plan to learn social skills or to compete in competitive obedience, a six-foot lead is what is required by most kennel clubs who offer dog performance sports competitions, so you will already have the only tool you really need if this is the lead you opt to purchase now. A six-foot lead provides your dog with lots of room to roam on a walk but is still short enough for it to focus on you. You will find the six foot-leash is an excellent length for teaching the "heel" position.

A long lead is a great tool for teaching your Cavapoo to have a solid recall. Leashes of 12 feet or longer allow your dog the opportunity to explore places further away from you but give you the security that the dog is still attached to you for safety.

Some people really love using flexible leads. This type of leash is retractable and varies in length from 16 ft to 26 ft. To use the flexible lead, find a field, and with a tight grip on the handle, you can let your pooch roam as far as the lead will allow it to go. It is a wonderful way to allow your dog to have the freedom to get in a run without compromising your need for your dog to remain safe. For best results, never use a Flexi in a dog park or on dog walks. Though Flexis are equipped with the ability to stop the lead at your desired length, a motivated dog could easily pull the Flexi handle out of your hand, and failure of the "halt" feature is also possible. Some owners panic when the "halt" option fails and attempt to grab the wire leash, causing deep cuts and painful abrasions to their hands.

## Cavapoo Harnesses—Is a Harness a Good Choice for a Cavapoo?

Harnesses can be an excellent alternative to using a collar on your Cavapoo. Though the Cavapoo is not a breed known for pulling, many dog owners feel the harness puts less stress on the trachea of the dog, making it a safer option to attach a leash to.

Harnesses come in several different styles. Some allow for the leash to be hooked in the middle of the back of the dog, while others are secured via the front. As with a collar, you will need to get the correct size in order for your harness to be an effective tool for your Cavapoo. If you do not obtain a proper fit, the harness will be uncomfortable for your dog and will rub against the skin causing cuts and abrasions. A harness that is too loose is a recipe for disaster if you have a Cavapoo Houdini who makes a habit of finding a way out of collars and harnesses.

## Cavapoo Kennels—How Do You Select the Right Size?

Since at some point in your Cavapoo's life it will need to be crated, it is always a good idea to buy a kennel or dog crate to use at home. Dog crates are an excellent means to assist with the housebreaking process. Many breeders like to begin crate training as early as five weeks old, so it may well be that your Cavapoo puppy is already very familiar with a crate and finds it a place of comfort. Whether you like to use a crate as your dog's bed, as a spot to contain them when you aren't at home, or even just a safe place to rest while traveling in the car, it is wise to teach your dog that a crate can be a great place to be. Undoubtedly at some point in your dog's life, it will need to remain in a crate while at the vet, so why not take the fear out of being crated now to help reduce stress later?

If you ever travel by air and wish to take your dog along, you will need to put your Cavapoo in a crate unless your dog is small enough to fit in a soft-sided carrier under an airplane seat in the cabin. The specifications required for airline travel in a cargo hold are very helpful in determining what size crate is the right fit for your Cavapoo. As a general guideline, airlines require you to purchase a kennel that has sufficient room for your dog to stand up, turn around, and lie back down. It is also preferable for the kennel to allow from 2"-4" of headspace.

Do be certain that the kennel is not too large to accommodate your dog's size well. If you use a crate for travel by car, a crate that is too large will jostle your dog around, which can harm your dog in the event of a collision.

## Cavapoo Dog Houses—How Do You Choose a Size and What Features Do You Need?

Cavapoos are a dog breed that loves the company of their families. For this reason, they are not a breed that would do well living outdoors. Still, it is always good to provide a space in your yard where your dog can retreat from the heat of the sun or the cool breezes of winter.

When you go shopping for a dog house for your Cavapoo, you will find all kinds of interesting styles to choose from. Many companies will manufacture a dog house to look like a miniature version of your own. But there is more to choosing your ideal Cavapoo dog house than style. One of the biggest considerations is selecting a dog house that will remain as clean and dry as possible on the inside. Since the purpose of your dog house is to give your dog an appropriate shelter in case of poor weather, its primary function is to keep your dog comfortable and dry. Be sure to choose one large enough to allow your dog to enter and exit the dog house with ease.

You will want to install comfortable bedding inside your Cavapoo's dog house. The best materials are ones that are absorbent. This rules out towels or blankets as they absorb moisture well, but they also retain it. Your best bet is using straw or hay.

If keeping your dog warm during outdoor activity is a concern, you can purchase heating pads to place inside the dog house. They provide an extra layer of insulation and comfort on cool days.

## Cavapoo Toys—What Selection Should You Make to Keep Your Dog Stimulated?

To keep your Cavapoo happy, you will need to provide regular physical and mental activity for your dog. Your Cavapoo is a very intelligent dog breed and will benefit from activities that keep its brain engaged and sharp.

The key to a happy Cavapoo is providing variety in their toys. This is simple to achieve by buying toys in a wide range of shapes, sizes, colors, and textures. Don't make the mistake of throwing all of your dog's toys into its toy box, then wondering why your dog seems bored within a few hours of receiving new toys! To keep your dog on their toes, only place a small number of toys in the toy box and rotate them out on a daily business. This will keep your dog's interest level piqued! Periodically, you can add something new into the mix to show your dog that now and then they just might find a special surprise in there. Like humans who tire of eating the same foods on a regular basis, so too do dogs tire of looking at the same old toys day in and day out.

You don't need to break the bank to find toys your Cavapoo will love. Purchase some high-quality items for your favorite dog store, but also take care to mix in a few odds and ends from the local department store. Add into the mix some rubber treat toys which can be stuffed with delicious treats then frozen to maximize chewing satisfaction. You can even introduce items like empty toilet paper rolls stuffed with treats then sealed shut to provide a brain game with a high-value food reward inside for your dog to puzzle out.

Another item your Cavapoo will enjoy is puzzle toys. Things like treat balls are a great item to keep your dog engaged. Your dog solves the "problem" then gets an awesome reward for their efforts. What could be better?

When selecting toys for your Cavapoo, there are a few caveats. Be especially careful to only purchase toys that are up to the task of being attacked by your Cavapoo's teeth. If you've got a pooch with the chewing strength of ten Cavapoos, you will need to buy only toys that are extremely durable and less likely to splinter into pieces that could be swallowed to cause an obstruction or choking hazard. It is also important that you select toys that are intended for dog use. Many children's toys seem similar to dog toys but are not built to withstand a dog's chewing.

Always buy toys that are appropriate to your Cavapoo's size.

## Cavapoo Dog Treats—How Do You Choose Safe and Yummy Snacks for Your Cavapoo?

Most Cavapoos love food, so you won't have any trouble finding something your dog will enjoy devouring! However, not all food is suitable for a dog to eat. It is always a good idea to do your homework to select dog treats that are tasty, but also healthy and nutritious for your Cavapoo to enjoy. There are many treats on the market today, but not all of them are a great choice for your dog.

Sadly, retailers know that dogs are attracted to treats and chews that are placed at the dog's eye level. Yet some of these items are not great choices for dogs and are best left on the shelf.

Some of the treats to avoid include:

- **Rawhides**

  There is no question that dogs do love rawhides. However, rawhides are chemically treated with harsh solutions in order to render them flexible enough to shape into easy to chew items for dogs. These solutions are also responsible for taking edible hides with a best before the expiration date and prolonging that through a process which makes them shelf-stable. These chemical concoctions are dangerous for our dogs, and in truth, the rawhide itself is also problematic. To keep a rawhide shelf-stable, it is treated with preservatives and antibiotics, some of which have been discovered to contain traces of the highly toxic arsenic.

  But more than this, rawhide is difficult for dogs to digest. These same chemical solutions that create a chew to provide long-lasting chewing satisfaction also prevent the product from breaking down in the dog's intestinal system. Perhaps even more seriously, when rawhide comes in contact with liquids, it can swell, leading to painful, and often serious, stomach problems.

- **Hooves**

  Hooves undergo a similar chemical process to rawhides. To adequately clean and sanitize hooves for canine consumption, the hooves are treated with insecticides, bleaches, and harsh chemicals. These solutions render the hoof "clean," but most certainly not safe.

  By nature, hooves are hard and have led to tooth breakage in dogs.

- **Pig's ears**

  Dogs love pig's ears! Unfortunately, they also land themselves on the no-no list when it comes to items to give your Cavapoo to enjoy. Pig's ears are exceedingly high in fat content. Too much fat in a dog's diet is a leading contributor to the painful condition known as pancreatitis.

  In a similar fashion to hooves and rawhides, pig's ears also receive the royal chemical treatment to help keep them preserved and clean.

  Pig's ears are also known to splinter into sharp pieces, which could potentially cause painful rips or tears in your dog's throat, stomach, or mouth.

The truth is dogs love treats, and we take great pleasure in providing them with things that bring them joy. With a few guidelines in place, you can definitely source some treats that are sure to bring your pooch a lot of excitement and chewing satisfaction. The best course of action is to choose treats which are made from natural ingredients whenever possible. Some preservatives are necessary to keep a product from quick spoilage; however, focus on purchasing treats that keep the additives to the bare minimum. The fewer ingredients on the list that you don't understand, the better.

When selecting treats, choose two different kinds for two very different jobs. When you are training, you will need to have small treats that are extremely attractive to your dog. Trainers refer to these as high-value treats. You will want to keep these small, even bite-sized, if possible. The small size keeps the calories from adding up quickly if you need to dispense a lot of them to reward the behavior you want to see in a training session. They must also be high value as you want to keep your dog motivated to work for you. Keep these treats specifically for training sessions only, so your dog learns to associate them with a very special reward. If you use them for everyday treats, they will very quickly lose their appeal.

You will also want to purchase a treat of lower value that you can use to give your Cavapoo, just because. These treats are used to reward learned behavior or just because your dog is cute, and you think they deserve a treat.

Here are some safe and yummy treats you can give to your Cavapoo:

- **Biscuit-like treats**

  Biscuit treats are also known as hard biscuits. They are a little tougher to chew, but that isn't a bad thing as they can also help keep plaque on your dog's teeth at bay. These treats are perfect to have on hand on a dog walk as they won't fall apart in your pocket. Use them to reinforce a job well done, to redirect attention on a walk, or even to train a new skill. Hard biscuits often require more than one bite, so they are not the ideal candidate for longer training sessions where a one bite treat is optimal.

  You will find many different cookbooks which offer recipes for making your own dog treats. These are biscuits your dog is sure to find delicious, but they often require refrigeration to keep from spoiling since they are free from chemicals and preservatives.

- **Soft treats**

  Most dogs love soft treats. They are wonderful tools for teaching your dogs to accept a treat with a soft mouth simply because grabbing at it will reduce a soft treat to crumbs.

  Like homemade hard biscuits, soft treats require refrigeration to enrich their shelf life and prevent mold formation. Soft treats are often stinky and tasty, making them a Cavapoo favorite.

- **Small, training treats**

  Every Cavapoo home must have small, training treats. You want to keep these treats bite-sized, so you can dispense them as often as you need to without fear of weight gain. Training treats should be the yummiest treats in your arsenal to keep your Cavapoo willing to work for more!

  You can find many different online recipes for training treats such as tuna fudge and liver cake. These treats are the ideal texture for slicing into small portions for training sessions. They are fragrant and delicious and will keep your pup wishing your training exercises would never end.

- **Dehydrated meats**

  Dehydrated meats are another excellent option to use as treats. You can buy many different dehydrated meat products at high-quality pet retailers. It doesn't matter whether you purchase lamb lung, tripe, or even liver, your pooch will love them all! Dogs love dehydrated meats! With so many to choose from, you can buy a few different varieties for your dog to sample then stock up on their favorite.

- **Appropriate people food**

  People food is particularly attractive to pooches. Care must be taken in selecting only foods that are appropriate for canine consumption, as some human foods are toxic to dogs. When it comes to people food, each dog is an individual when it comes to what they like. Some dogs will do backflips for a piece or broccoli while others hold out for prime rib trimmings. You can feel free to feed your dog people food but only in moderation to avoid gastrointestinal distress or pancreatitis. Also bear in mind that the more people food you give your dog, the greater the risk of your pooch becoming a picky eater who no longer thinks their kibble is worthy of them.

## Cavapoo Muzzles—How Do You Make Sure the Muzzle Fits?

Though muzzles have long been associated with aggressive dogs, they do serve a valuable purpose. It is a great advantage to your Cavapoo for your dog to feel comfortable wearing a muzzle. Starting early to get your dog accustomed to having a muzzle on is a skill that may come in handy later in life if the dog needs to be muzzled for its own protection.

Muzzles can be excellent tools to aid with everything from inhibiting barking to facilitating grooming procedures. You can even use a muzzle to protect your vet or to keep yourself from being bitten when your pooch is experiencing pain. Muzzles certainly have their practical uses, and it is worthwhile to "shape" your dog to accept a muzzle when one would be beneficial.

To be most effective, a muzzle must fit properly. Here is the best way to ensure your Cavapoo's muzzle fits correctly:

- With your dog's mouth open at a pant, measure the distance around your dog's snout from the widest point (closest to the eyes).

- Measure the distance from the bridge of the nose to the tip. This measurement will tell you the length you require.
- Measure the height from the tip of the nose to the bottom of the jaw.

Armed with these three measurements, you are sure to find the correct fit for your Cavapoo. The next step is to travel to your local pet store. You will want to bring your Cavapoo with you as measurements are a good guide, but there is no substitute for fitting a muzzle on the dog itself to be certain of a correct fit. Your dog should still be able to pant and move their mouth within reason.

When you go to purchase a muzzle, you will see that there are two different styles. There is one muzzle whose primary purpose is to restrict movement. This type of muzzle is designed to prevent bites. It is most effectively used during grooming sessions where the dog would be resistant to things such as bathing or having their nails clipped. This type of muzzle should only be used for a short period of time. It is formally known as an occlusion muzzle. Because it restricts panting, it should only be kept on until the grooming session is complete and always only with complete supervision.

If your dog needs to be muzzled for a longer period of time, a basket muzzle is the muzzle of choice. This type of muzzle does not restrict mouth movement. Instead, it simply removes access to the dog's mouth. The dog can still perform all of its normal basic functions such as panting, drinking, and barking. The only thing the dog cannot do is bite.

# CHAPTER 7

# Cavapoo Needs — Taking Care of Your Cavapoo

Every dog has needs, and it is important to understand the unique requirements of caring for a Cavapoo before bringing one to join your home. This is where your breeder's expertise will be especially helpful. Reputable breeders can enlighten you as to any particular "quirks" the breed may possess, and what you can expect. They will also be available to you for the life of the dog, giving you the opportunity to keep them involved in your dog's development and life achievements. It is to your advantage to build a strong and healthy relationship with your Cavapoo breeder. It will benefit you, and it will also greatly benefit your puppy.

*Your Cavapoo puppy is going to need lots of regular activity
to stay mentally and physically satisfied.*

## Basic Care of the Cavapoo

Having studied this book up to this point, you are likely already quite familiar with the basic care required for a Cavapoo puppy. You already know that you need to purchase the best quality food that you can afford and that you must provide regular veterinary care, which also includes vaccinations and flea, tick, and heartworm preventatives. As an excited new owner, you've already

91

gone to all the different pet stores to pick up every item on your list of supplies. But is there more to caring for your new pooch than you are prepared for?

## Common Cavapoo Health Issues

Cavapoos are not known to be predisposed to many health issues. The most common problems seen in the breed include mitral valve disease, hip dysplasia, and patellar luxation.

Genetic health issues which can plague both the Cavalier King Charles Spaniel, the Poodle, and the offspring of the two will be further discussed in a subsequent chapter.

## Cavapoo Puppies—What Do You Need to Know?

Caring for a Cavapoo puppy really is no different than caring for a puppy of any other breed. Your Cavapoo puppy will need training, as all puppies do. This training will help your puppy to learn its place in your home and what expectations you have for it. It is at this time that your Cavapoo puppy will also learn appropriate canine manners. Socialization and puppy obedience classes can form an integral part of your puppy training strategy. These types of classes can set forth simple criteria that can help enhance your training efforts. Best of all, training classes expose your puppy to novel experiences in an environment where a positive experience is ensured. This will help your puppy in its social development immeasurably.

As with all training exercises, consistency is the key to learning new skills. Your Cavapoo puppy will be most content when it has a thorough understanding of the boundaries in which it is to operate. It is equally as important for you to teach your Cavapoo that when you ask for a behavior, your puppy is expected to offer it at the time of the first request. A highly intelligent breed which is driven to please, the Cavapoo will not resist your training efforts and will actually be eager to spend its time learning new lessons and practicing established ones with you.

Positive reinforcement training is a technique that is particularly effective with the sweet-natured Cavapoo. This type of training focuses on the use of treats and praise to train a desired command or action from a dog. Those who support this method believe that its techniques build confidence in dogs and help them to learn to look forward to training opportunities. Positive reinforcement methodology supports a rewarding of good behavior with treats and praise and ignoring the bad. It is asserted that over time your dog will naturally repeat the behaviors that have been rewarded in the past and eliminate the ones that did not yield a treasure.

## How Much Exercise Does a Cavapoo Need?

How much exercise a Cavapoo puppy requires is not an easy question to answer. The truth is balance should always be the governing principle when it comes to any puppy and their daily activity allowance. Since a puppy has no idea of how activity affects them, they will go all day long if allowed to do so. However, as an owner, it is your responsibility to protect your dog from things that would cause it harm.

Both the use of the brain and the body lead to a dog that is fatigued. With it taking approximately 18 months for a Cavapoo's growth plates (bones which are connected with cartilage and muscle upon full maturity) to bond together, it becomes that much more important for the dog to be restricted to only moderate activity. Rigorous exercise such as long hikes or walks should be avoided until the dog is developmentally stable. To ignore this advice is to take unnecessary risks with your dog's structure and could lead to a serious injury that may possibly be debilitating for life. Yes, the Cavapoo was designed to enjoy moderate activity. The key is waiting until the appropriate age (after 18 months of age) to properly enjoy it.

With this in mind, moderation is the recommended route when it comes to exercise for the Cavapoo puppy. A walk which does not exceed thirty minutes per day and which traverses over level ground is perfectly acceptable for a pup under the age of 18 months. If this amount of exercise seems insufficient to meet your pup's needs, it is best to increase the number of walks per day instead of increasing duration or intensity.

To balance out your pup's need to be mentally and physically satisfied, it is a great idea to give your pooch some puzzle toys or interactive games to play with. This will help to tire out your puppy's active brain.

# CHAPTER 8

# Cavapoo Grooming—How Much Grooming Does a Cavapoo Require?

With a Cavapoo as part of your family, regular grooming will become a part of your normal routine. You will also need to find a professional groomer who can competently address the maintenance of your Cavapoo's coat. The Cavapoo requires much less coat work than other hybrids such as the Aussiedoodle or the Labradoodle. Still, regular brushing and grooming appointments are necessary to keep your dog's coat mat and tangle-free. Though Cavapoos can be born with a low-shedding coat, this is not always the case. To keep your Cavapoo's coat in proper condition, you will need to invest the time and effort in keeping it looking in tip-top shape. Failure to keep up with brushing your Cavapoo can result in your dog's coat needing to be completely shaved to remove any matting. This process is very uncomfortable for your dog at best. If you feel that this type of coat maintenance is beyond what you have the time for, the Cavapoo may not be the best breed for you.

## The Average Cavapoo Price for Grooming

The Cavapoo should see a groomer a minimum of three times per year. Assuming you keep up with regular brushing of your dog and keep your Cavapoo's coat mat and knot-free, you can expect to pay around $55 each visit to the grooming shop.

## Cavapoo Grooming Basics

The best thing you can do to get your Cavapoo puppy primed for regular grooming is to start desensitizing your dog to the necessary tools early. Many breeders help with this process by getting puppies up on the table as early as five weeks of age. This is the ideal time to introduce a dog to things like slicker brushes and combs, which will play a role in their regular grooming routine. Teaching your Cavapoo that grooming is a regular part of life and can be a positive experience is a great way to get your dog ready for its visits to a professional grooming shop.

When it comes to nail care, many breeders and groomers like to make use of a rotary tool known as a Dremel. This handheld sanding tool helps to keep the nails short and has the added bonus of making light work of the job and preventing painful nicks of the quick, which can cause the puppy to bleed. If begun in the breeder's home, your Cavapoo puppy should come to you already accustomed to the Dremel and ready for you to simply pick up where your breeder left off. If this is the case with your breeder, ask them to give you a quick demonstration so you can observe the process. One quick trip to the hardware store to purchase a Dremel all your own, and you are ready to go!

Some families and professional groomers prefer guillotine-style nail clippers, as pictured below. Dogs tend to be more resistant to this approach as it is much easier to cut the nails too short, causing pain and bleeding. However, with practice and skill, you can become quite adept at using nail clippers to keep your dog's nails neat and tidy.

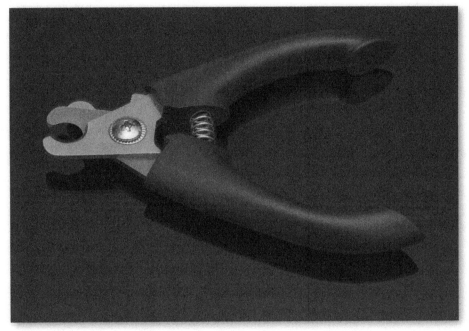

*Guillotine style clippers are very popular.*

As mentioned above, regular brushing is not optional if you are the owner of a Cavapoo. Failure to brush your dog several times a week will result in painful mats and knots in your dog's coat which are nearly impossible to work out with a comb. Even missing a day or two can lead to a coat that is beyond repair, meaning shaving will be necessary.

But beyond regular brushing, the Cavapoo's coat is low maintenance for you as the dog's owner. Your dog will need to see a groomer several times a year to keep its coat in good condition. But beyond that, the Cavapoo really is an easy breed to keep looking good.

Your groomer offers a number of services for your Cavapoo including:

- **Regular ear cleaning**

  Ear cleaning is a specialized skill. Great care must be taken to do it properly, or you can cause injury and intense pain to your dog. If you plan to clean your dog's ears yourself, it is best to ask your veterinarian to give you a lesson at your next visit. Your veterinarian will also sell the appropriate ear cleaning fluid you should use to keep your dog's ears sparkling clean. Under no circumstances should you ever insert any object, including Q-tips, into your dog's ear.

- **Tooth brushing or scaling**

  Keeping your dog's teeth clean is a vital part of ensuring your dog remains healthy. Many veterinarians provide their clients with a sample toothbrush and toothpaste to use on their dog. Unfortunately, most dogs do resist having their teeth brushed, but it is an important part of keeping your dog's teeth healthy.

  Your Cavapoo can become accustomed to having its teeth brushed if you approach doing it a little bit at a time. To do this, approach your dog with the toothbrush and gingerly brush a few teeth, paying particular attention to the gum line. When your dog allows you to brush those few teeth, praise your dog and give them a treat. That's enough for today. You can try a little more tomorrow. Over time, your pup will come to associate tooth brushing with its normal routine and will look forward to the treat it receives at the end.

For dogs with a more stubborn plaque problem, consider buying a dental scaler from a pet store. This will allow you to remove plaque away from the gums. This simple act will help prevent any bacteria or debris which could harbor there and begin the spread of periodontal disease.

- **Nail care and maintenance**

  Keeping your dog's nails short is an important part of maintaining proper foot health. You will find more information above regarding the proper care of your dog's nails.

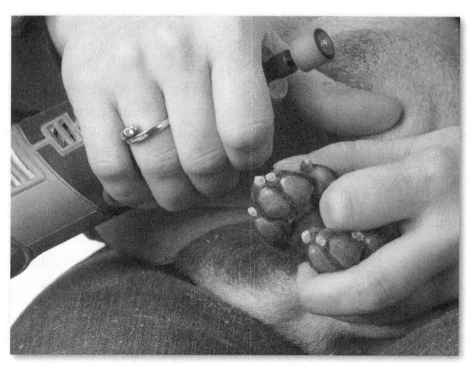

*A Dremel tool is a great way to keep your Cavapoo's nails nice and short.*

## Cavapoo Shampoos

Your groomer can provide excellent recommendations regarding the best products to use to keep your Cavapoo's coat healthy and clean. For the most part, you will not need to bath your Cavapoo at home, so using a dog shampoo will be a far rarer occurrence than with a higher maintenance breed.

Be certain to only purchase and use a shampoo that was intended for use on dogs. Many shampoos intended for human hair contain items which are not safe for use on pets. Human hair and dog hair are markedly different and require different shampoo formulations to safely bring out the best in each hair type.

When you are on the hunt for a shampoo for your Cavapoo, take the necessary time to read the label on each bottle. It is important to know what is in the product you plan to buy. If you come across a shampoo which does not list the ingredients, it is best to move on to another type of shampoo. Some shampoos contain chemicals which will improve coat quality but have the potential to make your dog ill. No product is worth that. It is recommended that you avoid shampoos containing these extremely toxic chemicals: include formaldehyde, sulfates, isopropyl alcohol, artificial colorings, and parabens.

With these facts in mind, it is best to avoid any products sold at department stores or pet suppliers. Your groomer is your best resource for high quality, safe shampoos for your pet.

## Cleaning a Dirty Cavapoo

Cleaning a dirty Cavapoo is really no different than cleaning any other breed. A dirty Cavapoo needs a bath! Armed with your pet-safe shampoo, you can hose down your fave pooch, lather, rinse, and repeat as necessary. It is always a good idea to use a pet-friendly leave-in conditioner on your Cavapoo's coat and to blow dry the dog to protect the integrity of the coat. Be sure to use a brush to rake through the hair as you blow dry. This will prevent knots from forming.

## Cavapoo Shedding—Do Cavapoos Shed?

Yes, Cavapoos do shed. However, they typically shed less than most breeds. How much your Cavapoo will shed depends on which side of its pedigree it favors most. If your Cavapoo more closely resembles its Cavalier King Charles Spaniel parent in coat type and texture, you will see far more hair shed into the environment than if your dog bears more of the genes from the Poodle.

## Are Cavapoos Hypoallergenic?

There is no such thing as a hypoallergenic dog. All dogs shed. In reality, people who react to the presence of animal hair are not , in fact, allergic to the hair. Their allergic reaction is to dander. Dander is simply the pet version of dandruff. Dead skin cells and saliva become trapped in the hair of the dog. When a dog sheds, this dander is then emitted into the environment inducing an allergic response in the allergy sufferer.

Unfortunately, all animals have dander, including dogs and cats. Dogs who shed less frequently may induce less of an allergic response from their owners. It is believed that since dander is trapped against the skin of dogs with low-shedding properties that the absence of dander in the home and in the air helps alleviate the suffering of those with a dander allergy.

## Finding a Professional Groomer for Your Cavapoo

Finding a professional groomer who understands what you are looking for in the grooming of your dog can be quite the challenge. Your breeders can often recommend a few different grooming shops you can try.

Other possible resources include other Cavapoo owners, social media platforms, or an online search.

# CHAPTER 9

# Cavapoo Training— Successfully Training Your Cavapoo

Since Cavapoos are a breed that loves to learn, you will have a ball training your new canine bundle of joy! Cavapoos possess a high desire to please their owners, so they are up for any training exercise on your agenda. The Cavapoo thrives under positive reinforcement training techniques. Positive reinforcement training can be done anywhere. All you need is a clicker and some yummy treats, and you're good to go!

*Cavapoos require some training. What could be better than playtime with a friend for a reward after a session?*

## What Tools Do You Need for Cavapoo Training?

The best thing about positive reinforcement training for your Cavapoo is you really need only a few tools to get you started. Your local pet store will have everything you need. Just load up on some super yummy treats and buy a clicker, and you're ready to train!

## What Treats Are Good for Positive Reinforcement Training for Your Cavapoo?

The treats you buy will largely be dependent upon your Cavapoo's unique tastes. Regardless of what you choose, the one common factor must be the treats are small, and the bite-sized ones are preferable. To teach a new behavior or reinforce an old one, you will need to dispense a large number of treats to aid in the learning process. The best training treats are small, soft, low in calories, and extremely delicious.

For this reason, many families like to use recipes for homemade treats such as liver cake or tuna fudge. Easy to find on the internet, these recipes make a large yield that can then be cut into the appropriate size for training.

Some owners like to make use of cat treats. Cat treats are known to be the perfect size. They are typically crunchy and have the added bonus of being low calorie. They are also rather fragrant, making them appealing to a Cavapoo on a mission to learn new skills.

If you're out of treats but still want to train, you just might find the perfect thing housed within your fridge. Most Cavapoos love any meat or cheese. Simply raid your fridge to find hidden treasures, then cut your finds into small, bite-sized pieces, and you're off to the races!

Why do you need high value treats for training? Dogs love to eat. But dogs also become accustomed to foods we give them as rewards. Over time, the treat that used to elicit a joyful response will become ho-hum if received on a regular basis. If you love to give your dog a treat "just because," you don't have to stop doing this. Instead, stock your house with treats for everyday use and treats that are reserved specifically for training. When it comes to teaching new behaviors, it is always a good idea to have a little added food incentive on your side!

## What Does Your Cavapoo Need to Learn?

All dogs need proper canine skills to navigate their world successfully. Learning canine manners and obedience commands have the potential to save your dog from harm and could even save your Cavapoo's life. With this in mind, every Cavapoo should learn the most basic obedience commands.

Positive reinforcement training makes learning a new skill lots of fun! To teach your Cavapoo a new skill, all you will require is a clicker and some treats. To give you a basic example as a guideline, we will discuss how to teach your Cavapoo the **"sit"** command. When you want your dog to **"sit,"** hold a treat above the head of your dog. Dogs will naturally move their bodies into a **"sit"** position when something is above their head in order to gain a better view of it. When your dog moves to the correct position, you give a quick click of your clicker and immediately furnish the treat. In this manner, your dog learns that the correct action equals a reward. Some dogs may resist sitting, and if they do, you can gently help them along by using your hand to delicately lower your dog into the correct position. When your dog is seated, you should name the behavior as a **"sit"** to help your dog learn what you expect when you say that word. You can then click and reward your dog. Repeat this behavior a few more times to reinforce your Cavapoo's learning. Your dog will master this command rather quickly, but that doesn't mean you should stop asking your Cavapoo for it during training sessions on a periodic basis. It is always good to reinforce previously learned commands to ensure they remain a solid part of your dog's trick repertoire. Over time, you can phase out treats entirely and just lavish your dog with praise for a job well done.

Here are the skills your Cavapoo needs to know to live a safe and happy life:

- "Sit"

  As previously discussed, the **"sit"** command is relatively simple to train as it is a natural default position for most dogs. Since sitting is a comfortable activity for dogs, they are already familiar with the action, meaning you just have to name it and reinforce it with treats and praise for your dog to understand what you want when you ask for it. Teaching a **"sit"** is important as from time to time, you will want your dog to **"sit"** quietly. Some occasions where the **"sit"** command is helpful is when exiting a door or when waiting to receive a treat. **"Sit"** is also often used as a foundation skill for learning other more intricate commands such as **"down"** and **"stay."**

- Down or flat

  The **"down"** command is a very useful skill for all dogs to have. At times, you will want your dog to fully recline when asked to do so. Whether you use the name **"down"** or **"flat"** is entirely up to you. Whichever word you choose, be consistent as your Cavapoo will be easily confused if you use the two terms interchangeably while training.

- Come

  The command **"come,"** which is also referred to as a recall, is a vital skill every Cavapoo needs to know. The **"come"** command is not optional as it is the one skill in your dog's command arsenal that has the potential to save your dog's life. **"Come"** should be taught alongside the **"stay"** command as the ability to **"sit"** then **"stay"** could keep your dog safe from injury, accident, and even death in an emergency situation.

You will have some victories and some setbacks in teaching this command. But whether your dog comes to you the first time you ask for it or the fifth, it is essential that when your dog comes to you that it is time to party! If you scold your dog for not coming the first time they were called, your dog will associate its decision to finally come to you with your displeasure, and this could negatively impact your training efforts. Always be certain that when your dog comes to you, it is an occasion for celebration! To be certain your dog's recall is solid, it is important that you practice the **"come"** command in a variety of different locations and under distraction. Dogs do not generalize well so the Cavapoo that will **"come"** to you in your backyard might have no idea what you expect them to do if you ask for the same command in the parking lot of your local grocery store. A reliable recall takes much practice and much effort, but it is worth every minute expended to teach it.

- **Off**

  Though most people consider the Cavapoo, a lap dog, it is still important for your dog to understand that they must get off someone when asked to do so. Failure to remove themselves from a person when it is requested of a dog is extremely poor canine manners.

- **Leave it**

  Cavapoos can be mischievous little creatures, and that is where the **"leave it"** command comes in. Since dogs love to explore their world with their mouths, they can put all kinds of things in there, some of which are harmful to them. The **"leave it"** command gives you the opportunity to ask your dog to refrain from touching something that could cause the dog injury or harm.

- Out

  Sometimes our dogs get to an object before we can use the **"leave it"** command, so we have to up the ante to using **"out."** Teaching an **"out"** command gives you the ability to request your dog relinquish an item to you immediately when asked to do so. A critical part of teaching this skill is making sure you always replace the object your dog gives up with something much, much better; otherwise, your Cavapoo may become resentful of you or simply refuse to relinquish their prize.

- Heel

  Though not all owners like their dogs to heel on a walk, it is still an excellent skill for all dogs to learn. There will be times when you want your dog's focus to remain on you, and the heel position is the ideal to accomplish this. If your dog is reeled out six feet ahead of you, it is very difficult for them to be paying attention to you. But more than that, the basis for all leash manners is found in learning to **"heel."**

## How Do You Deal with Unwanted Cavapoo Behaviors?

There is always an adjustment period when it comes to learning new skills. Your Cavapoo may also develop some behaviors you don't like along the way. No one likes naughty behavior from their dog so it will be important to address these issues before they become something you see on a regular basis.

The first step to dealing with unwanted behaviors is to gird yourself up to be patient during the learning process. The behavior most likely did not appear overnight, and it is not going to disappear in one session either. Your patience during your training efforts will be greatly rewarded.

The second important step you must undertake is assessing what might be motivating this behavior in your Cavapoo. Is it possible that your dog is unwell? Has there been a change in your home that is causing your dog to act out? Is this a recent behavior, or has it been simmering under the surface for some time, and you're just finding it annoying now? What is your dog's age? Could your dog be experiencing a fear period that is affecting their behavior? The answer to these questions is important in helping you to understand how to best help your dog.

When trying to eliminate a nuisance behavior, it is always a good idea to go back to the basics. You may think your dog has mastered all of its commands, but it never hurts to undergo a refresher.

A vital step is to never, EVER reward the behavior you are trying to eradicate. No matter how adorable your dog might look engaging in the behavior you don't like, you must stay strong and refuse to even hint at any pleasure from what your dog is doing. Your Cavapoo is a very smart little dog, and all dogs learn quite young to repeat behavior that gives them what they see as a payoff. Rewards don't have to come in the form of treats or praise. For your Cavapoo, the reward could simply be the hint of a smile on your face or a laugh you didn't intend to let slip. You must learn to master a "poker face" to be an effective dog trainer, or you will soon find your dog is training you!

Consistency is always the key to learning. You must remain firm and consistent to eliminate behavior you don't want to see in your dog. To allow it one day than to not tolerate the next is unfair to your Cavapoo and sets them up for confusion and frustration.

As a gentle-natured breed, it is important that all re-training efforts be based on positive reinforcement methods. The Cavapoo loves to please, and to use aversive training tools such as shock collars could be harmful to your dog's spirit as well as its bond with you. If you are properly employing the techniques of positive reinforcement yet still not seeing desirable results, your best course of action is to contact a reputable behavior modification specialist to assist you.

## How Do You Properly Socialize Your Cavapoo?

Cavapoos are a friendly breed. Since they are known as canine gentlemen, their manners are so impeccable that they are unlikely to offend other dogs or people that they meet. Still, all dogs do require proper socialization to learn to navigate their world well.

Since Cavapoos are naturally both curious and friendly, you will find your pooch is only too happy to accompany you wherever you want to go. Still, since it is impossible to know exactly what your Cavapoo experienced at the breeder's house, you will want to take your Cavapoo to see all of the different things that they will be involved in in their new home. Even the friendliest dog in the world can develop shyness if not given ample opportunity to experience novel things in a positive environment.

The main things you will want to socialize your Cavapoo to, are the following:

- **Children**
- **Loud or unusual noises**
- **New environments**
- **Novel surfaces**
- **Other animals**
- **Adults**

The majority of your Cavapoo's socialization will be undertaken at your breeder's home. However, before your puppy reaches 16 weeks of age, you have a valuable opportunity to introduce him to novel experiences which will help reinforce its confidence. Research shows that puppies learn the majority of what they will ever know prior to reaching 16 weeks of age. If you are wise, you will make the most of this important emotional and social developmental period in your Cavapoo's life. Your dog will still continue to learn things once they have passed week 16; however, they are not as easily impressionable after this time. With a puppy being like a sponge for learning in the first 16 weeks of life, it cannot be overstated how important it is to keep all interactions and new experiences positive. While positive experiences will have a lifelong positive impact on your dog during this phase, negative situations also leave a lasting mark. If you cannot be certain the outing you have in mind will end well, DO NOT TAKE YOUR PUPPY.

Always keep an eye on your Cavapoo when introducing them to new things. If your dog is reacting poorly, do not force the dog to engage with the person or object that is causing it distress. Let your dog be your guide when it comes to socialization experiences. If you force your dog to approach something that is upsetting them, you will reinforce the fear as well as teach your dog that they can't trust you to keep them safe.

You can also socialize your dog to unusual noises. There are lots of audio clips available on online video sites which allow you to expose your dogs to such things as babies crying, a noisy puppy class, thunderstorms, police sirens, and much more. For best results, you can play these audio clips while your dog is relaxing at home. Eventually, the dog will simply accept the sounds as normal and be completely unaffected by them.

Bear in mind that all dogs experience fear periods. When your Cavapoo is entering a fear period, it is best to make their world smaller and cease socialization opportunities as they could do more harm than good at this time. Sometimes puppies in a fear period will even appear to regress. They might pay no mind at all to your husband's favorite hat on Monday, and on Wednesday, it is now the scariest thing on earth. The main thing is to provide consistent support for your dog and continue on with business as usual until the fear period has passed. Most often, fear periods only last a few days or up to a week.

## Can You Train Your Cavapoo to Swim?

Cavapoos are a breed that enjoys the water. Since each dog is an individual, it is hard to say definitively if your pooch will love to swim. However, with the Poodle in its pedigree, it is quite possible. The main thing when it comes to Cavapoos and swimming is to allow your dog to make the decision for itself. If your Cavapoo is a water lover, you will find it hard to keep them out of the water. But if your dog tends to peruse the shore but avoid taking the plunge, water might not be for them. Give your Cavapoo the opportunity to decide for themselves if swimming is for them or not.

## Is It a Good Idea to Train Your Cavapoo with a Shock Collar?

Cavapoos are a sweet-natured, happy-go-lucky breed. Since they are hardwired from birth to want to please their owners, using a shock collar on them would be counterproductive, and even harmful, not only to the dog's nature but also to the training process as a whole. It is never recommended to use a shock collar on a Cavapoo.

# CHAPTER 10

# Cavapoo Breeding— Getting Your Cavapoo Ready for a Litter

Breeding your dogs can be very exciting. It also has the potential to be dangerous and scary, so it should never be undertaken lightly. If breeding is something you have on your mind, you must be certain to carefully do your research and to take all necessary steps to get your dog prepared. Breeding a very serious business. You are creating lives that you will be responsible for up to 15 years or more. But more than this, there are criteria that must be adhered to qualify a dog for breeding. The simple truth is for the health and future of the breed, not every dog should be bred. Many people think that every female dog should be permitted to have one litter to fulfill her natural maternal instincts. This is absolutely not true.

The first question you need to ask yourself if breeding is on your mind is: why do you want to breed your Cavapoo? Understanding your own personal motivations is key to helping you determine if breeding is the right choice for you and your dog. Creating a new business is never a good reason to become a breeder. The truth is very few reputable breeders ever make any money on their litters. In fact, most lose money and lots of it. You must also bear in mind that our world is currently experiencing a major pet overpopulation problem, and you don't want to contribute to that. Your dog might be the cutest thing to ever walk this earth, but that alone is not sufficient reason to breed your dog.

The next step is for you to take an honest look at your dog to determine what it is you feel your dog possesses that would be of value to future generations of the Cavapoo. Money is not a motivation for responsible breeders. Most reputable breeders breed to give back to a breed they have devoted their lives to helping preserve. Today, there are many backyard breeders who put no care into breeding two dogs together so long as it makes them a buck. This leads to breeds becoming so diluted that they no longer resemble the breed they should anymore. This becomes even more important with the Cavapoo who right now is still defining a standard for who and what they should look like. Still, appearance is the very last thing that reputable breeders concern themselves with, as important as it is. Indiscriminate breeding practices can lead to health conditions and a reoccurrence of genetic disease in puppies. This is a great heartbreak for not only the breeder but also for the breed and the future owners of those puppies.

Any dog who is used in a breeding program should have something to contribute to the gene pool of the breed. Because the Cavapoo is a mixed breed, this is slightly more complex to determine. With no definitive written standard in such a young breed, much inconsistency still prevails when it comes to appearance, temperament, and personality. For this reason, it is recommended that you apply your focus to two things: making certain your dogs are healthy and free from genetic disease, and that your dogs have solid temperaments.

Since temperament is largely inherited, an aggressive dog should never be bred. Even if every other quality that dog possesses is stellar, you cannot overlook a bad temperament. As previously stated, not all dogs should be bred. Only the very best examples of the breed should take pride of place in any breeding program. The two dogs you consider for breeding must display the most desirable traits in the ideal Cavapoo. This means selecting only dogs who are happy and sweet by nature and who love to please their people. These are hallmarks of the breed. You must always dismiss any dog that displays undesirable temperament traits such as hyperactivity, aggression, or neuroses. Always bear in mind that parent dogs often produce dogs with stronger traits than they themselves possess. Don't fall into the trap of hoping the temperaments will be better in future offspring. That is not how it works.

Since Cavapoos are not currently a recognized breed, this means that your puppies will be going to homes where they will live out their lives as much beloved pets. What does this mean? It means an emphasis on correct, sound temperament is even more important. When you breed dogs, you are making a commitment to stand behind your puppies and their owners for life. If you choose to breed together two dogs who are not of sound temperament, you are handing off liabilities to your owners. Many owners are not equipped to deal with the challenges of a "problem" dog, and you will find that dog back in your home for you to deal with, or worse…in a rescue. This is not a good situation for your dog, for you, or your puppies' owners. But this does not happen to you or to the puppies you breed. Avoid these problems by only breeding dogs with exceptional temperaments. A passable one is not sufficient. Only dogs with the very best temperaments should ever be bred.

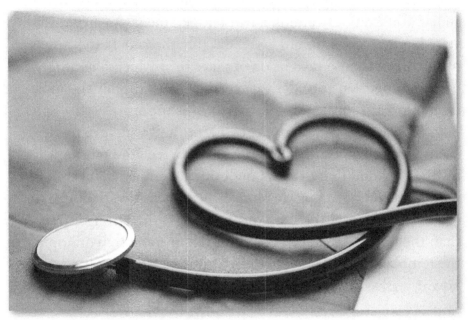

*Only Cavapoos who pass stringent health testing specific to their heritage should be bred.*

## Necessary Health Testing for Prospective Cavapoo Breeding Dogs

Once you have determined that you have selected two fine examples of the Cavapoo breed in both temperament and conformation, your next step is to complete all health testing. The best place to start is with a thorough wellness exam with your veterinarian. This will help to rule out any abnormalities or cause for concern in the outside appearance of your dog. However, a physical examination is not enough to approve a dog for breeding. Genetic illness and more serious physical problems can hide within your dog's inner workings. For this reason, you must strictly follow all health testing requirements for any potential inherited disease or physical problem which could befall the breed. What you are looking for is simple: if your dog does not pass, your dog should not be bred.

With all of this information in mind, it is quite easy to see that wanting your dog to have a litter simply on the merit of her being cute is not wise. Breeding dogs must be taken with the utmost of seriousness. You can run into many different complications during the breeding, whelping, and rearing process that you may be ill-equipped to handle. These unforeseen problems will cost you time, lots of money, and most of them will tear your heart into pieces. It is particularly heartbreaking to lose your female during whelping. In the midst of your grief, you will still have a litter of puppies needing your constant care. You must make yourself aware of all of the pros and cons before leaping into breeding your first litter.

Here are the health tests every potential Cavapoo breeding dog should undergo and pass in order to be considered for use in a breeding program:

- **CAER testing to rule out Progressive Retinal Atrophy (PRA), Collie Eye Anomaly (CEA), and cataracts**

  CAER stands for Companion Animal Eye Registry. This type of test is required to certify that a dog's eyes are normal and permits results to be listed on the Orthopedic Foundation for Animals, a service which records health testing with the owner/breeder's permission for the public to view. All Cavapoo breeding dogs should be certified as having normal eyes to be considered for a breeding program.

The main eye issues that can befall a Cavapoo are Progressive Retinal Atrophy, Collie Eye Anomaly, and cataracts. The Cavapoo gets a double whammy of PRA genes as both the Cavalier King Charles Spaniel and the Poodle can be prone to developing this disease. Progressive Retinal Atrophy is defined as a progressive deterioration of the retina. The disease is painful and eventually leads to blindness.

Collie Eye Anomaly is a hereditary defect affecting the integrity of the dog's eye. The condition can be minor or quite serious and can lead to vision impairment and even blindness.

Cataracts typically emerge shortly after birth or prior to a dog reaching three years of age. Cataracts in dogs most often do lead to blindness.

- **Echocardiogram to rule out Mitral Valve Disease**

  Mitral Valve Disease is common to both Cavalier King Charles Spaniels and Poodles, which makes it also common to the Cavapoo. Mitral Valve Disease, which is essentially an enlarging of the heart muscle causing heart murmurs, breathing difficulties, and possible fluid on the lungs, can be detected on an x-ray. Should Mitral Valve Disease be suspected, an echocardiogram is necessary to determine the extent of the illness in the dog. Any dog who presents with a heart issue is unsuitable for breeding.

- **OFA or Penn Hip testing for Hip and Elbow Dysplasia**

  If the femur joint of a dog does not rest properly in the hip socket, hip and elbow dysplasia is the result. Hips and elbows can be affected by nutrition and environmental factors, but the largest determining factor is the hip and elbow scores of a dog's parents. Both OFA and Penn Hip bestow "grades" or "scores" which reveal the extent of a dog's hip and elbow condition. These grades can range from a fail to fair, normal, good, and even excellent. You want to give great consideration to breeding a dog with only fair hips and elbows, and if you opted to do so, the dog should be bred only to other Cavapoos with good or excellent scores to improve the chances of producing good or excellent hips and elbows. Normal, good, or excellent grades are acceptable in Cavapoo breeding stock.

- **OFA Patella exam to test for Luxating Patellas**

  Luxating Patellas is another condition which is common to both the Cavalier King Charles Spaniel and the Poodle. A luxating patella is essentially knee cap that slips out of place. This condition is incredibly painful and can lead to excruciating tears of ligaments and tendons, which would require extensive surgeries to repair.

  The test for luxating patellas is quite simple and can be conducted by your veterinarian in his or her office. As with hips and elbows, patellas are given grades, but their scale is numeric. Only dogs with patellas that cannot be luxated are suitable for breeding.

- **Blood work to screen for Hypothyroidism and Pelger Huet Anomaly**

  An improperly functioning thyroid produces too little hormone. Hypothyroidism is genetic. Common symptoms include weight gain, excessive hunger, lethargy, and poor coat texture.

Pelger Huet Anomaly is a very rare genetic condition; however, all breeding dogs should be tested for the gene as it can cause jaw and skeleton deformities and issues with proper cartilage growth and development.

• **DNA testing for Von Willebrand's Disease**

DNA tests are quite simple. You order a set of swabs from a lab, take the swabs to the vet who then takes a sterile sample from your dog, and off the swabs go for processing. In several weeks, your lab of choice will contact you with the results.

Von Willebrand's Disease is a condition of the blood where a dog lacks the ability for its blood to clot properly.

These tests comprise a critical baseline from which you can assess whether or not your dog is suitable for breeding. Should your dog receive even a single failing score, it is best to remove them as an option in your breeding program. The future health and safety of the breed depend on it.

## The Female Cavapoo—Getting Ready for Breeding

If your female Cavapoo has passed all of her required health screening, it is now time to begin getting her ready for breeding. The appropriate age for a first litter is any time after two years of age. Some people do breed younger, but this is never advised. Allow your female to enjoy her puppy years and to grow into emotional maturity before allowing her to become a mother. This is best for your female and for her puppies.

Health testing can begin as young as one year of age. Bear in mind that some health tests are age-specific such as OFA hips, elbows, and patellas. The OFA website can provide specific information about the recommended ages for each test.

Your timing must be precise to ensure a viable litter. Females only cycle once or twice yearly. It is possible for pregnancy to occur any time during a heat cycle; however, there are certain times during that heat when females are primed for breeding. This typically takes place from as early as the 7th day to as late as the 10th day of the 30-day cycle. The only accurate measurement of optimal fertility is through using progesterone testing on a daily basis. You would normally begin this on Day 7. Most often; when your girl is willing to stand for a male, she is ready to conceive. Once this fertile period occurs, you will want to breed the two dogs every other day until the female is no longer willing to receive the male's attention. This offers you the best chances of a successful mating.

The common practice is for the female dog to be taken to the home of the stud dog for breeding.

There are no additional care requirements for a female dog prior to mating, assuming you have already been feeding her high-quality food and supplements to promote excellent health.

## The Male Cavapoo—Getting Ready for Breeding

By comparison, the stud dog should also be kept in prime health, and this begins with high-quality food. The main goal with stud dogs is keeping their sperm in optimal condition. Once a stud dog has passed all of his health testings, the next step is for your veterinarian to collect and analyze your dog's semen. This process should occur every so often to help clean out his system and ensure his semen remains fresh and vital.

Do take care that your home temperature is appropriate to allow your dog to brew strong sperm. Moderate temperatures are recommended. Extreme heat and cold should be discouraged.

## Sourcing a Good Quality Cavapoo Stud Dog

Perhaps the hardest part of the entire process is selecting the right dog to breed to your female. You will need to spend a good amount of time carefully considering the strengths and weaknesses of your female then finding a male who can balance these out in the breeding. When evaluating a stud dog, it is an excellent idea to look at the dogs who are behind him to best understand what genes came together to produce the dog you are currently looking at. These qualities may surface in the puppies.  Always remember that no dog is perfect. You are not looking for the perfect dog; you are looking for the ideal mate for your girl, a dog that will balance out her negative qualities with his positive ones.

Once you have determined your male of choice, you will then need to approach the dog's owner to see if they are willing to approve the potential mating. There is a fee that you will need to pay, which is most often the same amount as you would pay for a puppy. Some stud dog owners will opt instead to take the puppy of their choice from the litter instead of a stud payment. These are the factors the two of you can decide upon together.

The stud fee can be handled in several different ways. Some breeders want the payment upfront at the time of breeding. Others request a deposit with the balance paid at the time the puppies are whelped, or when they leave for their new homes. This is a personal matter and should be discussed and agreed upon ahead of time.

You will typically sign a contract prior to the breeding. The contract should clearly outline what each party is agreeing to, and it forms an agreement which is legally binding between the two of you. Your contract should very clearly outline what constitutes a "live breeding" (usually two puppies live at the time of birth) and what happens if the mating is unsuccessful. Most stud dog owners will offer you the option of a free repeat breeding should the first attempt be unfruitful.

## Newborn Cavapoo Puppies—Their Care and Feeding

Newborn Cavapoo puppies are very easy for you to care for. In fact, you will not be needed much at all as the mother dog does the majority of the work. While the mother dog takes the primary responsibility for the feeding and cleaning of her babies, you will be busy weighing and monitoring weights to ensure each puppy is growing. Your main role at this time is to take care of your mother dog to be sure she is thriving. At this time, your female will need high-quality nutrition and lots of it to continue to produce milk to feed her babies.

Around Day 12, the puppies' eyes will open. At this point, the puppies learn to urinate and defecate on their own, and your job begins! From this phase forward, you will be quite busy cleaning up puppy messes and preventing puppies from accidentally rolling or stepping in their own waste. It is also around this time that teeth erupt, and your female will lose interest in nursing. You will then need to begin introducing your puppies to gruel, which can then be transitioned to the eating of kibble once the full set of puppy teeth are in place.

You will also be very busy with socialization exercises to help the puppies learn what it means to be a dog in a human's world. You won't have much free time to yourself, but you will have fun, for sure. Puppies are with you for such a short time, you will want to spend as much time with them as possible.

# CHAPTER 11

# Cavapoo Lifestyle—What is it Like to Live with a Cavapoo?

There will be an adjustment period when it comes to getting used to living with a Cavapoo. Cavapoos are joy-filled little dogs who will add character and fun to your family. Still, it is always a good idea to understand ahead of time what life with a Cavapoo will be like!

*Life with a Cavapoo is always lots of fun!*

## Becoming a Savvy Cavapoo Owner

To have a great relationship with your Cavapoo, it is always a good idea to try to understand what makes them tick. Your Cavapoo is quite intelligent and has the energy to back up its smarts. This means the sky is limit when it comes to the adventures you can enjoy together!

## Getting Your House Ready for Your Cavapoo Puppy

All puppies coming into a new home will be mischievous. With this in mind, you will need to "puppy proof" your house. Take an honest look around your home and try to identify any items that might prove tempting to a Cavapoo puppy. Always bear in mind that to a Cavapoo puppy, pretty much anything is an opportunity for chewing fun! To keep your pooch safe, remove any items you don't want to be destroyed, or that could cause hurt to your dog. To keep your shoes intact, place them behind closet doors. It is also a good idea to keep all electrical items, not in use, unplugged.

Your Cavapoo will need to know where to go to find things like water and food bowls and its bed. For food and water dishes, choose a central location in your home. The best spot is a place that is easy for you and close to where the activity is as your Cavapoo will want to be wherever you are! Place dog beds in the place where you and your family spend the most time.

You will also need to pick up necessary items such as toys, a collar, and a leash. Until you know what types of toys your Cavapoo prefers, just buy a random sampling.

It is always good to decide ahead of time where your puppy will sleep at night. Some dog owners will allow their dogs to sleep in their beds. Others would rather the dog have a separate place all their own to enjoy. Make the decision where your Cavapoo will sleep and get the area ready for your new pooch's arrival.

## Are Cages a Good Idea for a Cavapoo?

As discussed in a previous chapter, cages, or crates, can be a great tool for your Cavapoo. However, it is important to take the time to teach your Cavapoo that their cage is a fun place to be, not a punishment. This is easy enough to do by providing fun rewards each time your dog needs to go to their cage.

Cages can also help you with the housebreaking process. But perhaps most importantly, your Cavapoo needs a safe space to retreat to when you cannot be home to provide supervision. A cage is the perfect solution!

Just be certain that if your dog needs to spend some time in their crate that you leave them with something fun to do while in there. This can be as simple as a treat ball, a bone, or a fun plush toy.

## Do You Need a Kennel for a Cavapoo?

If you do not have a securely fenced yard, an outdoor kennel might be a good solution for your Cavapoo. However, an outdoor kennel run as a containment option for long periods of time is not the best concept for a Cavapoo. Since this breed thrives on being with people, a Cavapoo left in an outdoor kennel may easily resort to a habit of regular nuisance barking.

If you opt to add an outdoor kennel to your yard, it is best used for periods of time when you are working outside, and your Cavapoo would like to be with you.

It is recommended that a Cavapoo never be left in a kennel run without supervision.

## Cavapoos and Dog Doors—Do You Need a Dog Door in Your Home?

Dog doors are easy to install and can make life much easier for you and your Cavapoo. However, a dog door should be accompanied by a fenced yard to keep your Cavapoo safe.

Before taking the plunge to add a dog door to your home, you will need to determine if your dog can be trusted in your backyard without supervision. If your Cavapoo is a master escape artist, this might not be a good plan for you.

If you do decide to install a dog door, be sure you can bar the door off from your Cavapoo when necessary. There will be times when you do not want your dog out in your yard, and having the ability to restrict your dog's access to the house will be important for you.

## Cavapoos and Dog Gates—Do You Need to Install a Dog Gate?

Dog gates give you the opportunity to keep your dog contained to a specific area of your home. These are a good idea for every dog owner's home as they serve a very practical purpose. If you want to keep your Cavapoo out of a room while you clean it, a baby gate is the perfect solution. You can mop away while your dog observes from their side of the gate!

## Should You Allow Your Cavapoo on Your Furniture?

This is really a personal decision. Some people allow their Cavapoos on all furniture in the home; others don't want the dog up at all. Whatever you decide, be consistent in teaching your dog the areas that are allowed, and which ones are not. Alternatively, it is possible to teach your Cavapoo that they are allowed on certain pieces of furniture when given permission. If you do teach this, you must also teach that the dog must get off the furniture when asked to do so and without complaint.

# CHAPTER 12

# Cavapoo Health— What Do You Need to Know?

I n general, the Cavapoo is a healthy breed. Still, all dog breeds are predisposed to certain health conditions, so it is a good idea to understand what problems are common to the Cavapoo.

## What are Common Cavapoo Health Problems?

Cavapoos really have very few genetic health problems. Discussed more in-depth in the chapter on breeding and necessary health testing, here is a list of known genetic diseases and physical problems which can befall a Cavapoo:

- Eyes—Progressive Retinal Atrophy, Collie Eye Anomaly, Cataracts
- Hip and Elbow Dysplasia
- Hearts—Mitral Valve Disease
- Luxating Patellas

- Endocrine Disorders--Hypothyroidism, Cushing's Disease

  These diseases affect the normal functioning and release of the thyroid hormone. If your dog presents with any of the symptoms of either disease, which can include hair loss, weight gain, and excessive lethargy, there is no cure. However, synthetic hormone therapy can help alleviate side effects and allow your dog to live a normal, happy life.

- Pelger Huet Anomaly

  Pelger Huet Anomaly is an extremely rare genetic disorder which affects proper development of the skeletal and musculature systems. There is no known treatment for this disease.

- Von Willebrand's Disease

  Von Willebrand's Disease is present when a dog lacks the correct enzyme for their blood to clot properly. There is no treatment for this disease; however, should your dog have an accident where there is a lot of blood loss incurred, a blood transfusion may be necessary.

  As Hypothyroidism, Cushings Disease, Pelger Huet Anomaly, and Von Willebrand's Disease are all genetic disorders; unfortunately, there is nothing that can be done to minimize the risks of developing them. The only course of action to prevent future generations from befalling these illnesses is to only breed dogs that have been DNA tested and received "clear" health results for each of the aforementioned disorders.

## Cavapoos and Bloat—Is Bloat a Problem for the Cavapoo?

Bloat is not typically an issue which affects Cavapoos.

Bloat is what occurs when fluid, food, or gas builds up around the stomach and causes the abdomen to inflate. This inflation increases pressure on vital organs which can lead to breathing obstructions, restricted blood flow to the heart and brain, or a rupture in the stomach. Bloat can lead to a condition known as torsion where the dog's intestines twist. This is a very painful ailment which most often results in death.

It is believed Bloat may be caused by the following factors:

- Eating only one large meal per day
- Consuming food or water for a raised dish
- Eating too quickly
- Rigorous activity directly after eating
- Genetic predisposition
- Anxiety

## What Vaccinations Will Your Cavapoo Need?

All dogs require regular vaccinations. It is recommended that you seek your breeder and your veterinarian's advice in making these decisions for your Cavapoo. Typically, at age eight weeks and just prior to your puppy joining your family, your puppy should receive its first shot in a three-shot series which is then boostered at age one year. This series of vaccinations piggybacks on any remaining maternal antibodies your puppy will have from consuming its mother milk and will reinforce and support the antibodies already at work in your puppy's body. This three vaccination series of shots should include the following immunizations:

- Distemper
- Adenovirus
- Parvovirus
- Parainfluenza

This initial series of shots is known as DA2PP and is commonly referred to as a puppy's core vaccines. These shots are most commonly administered several weeks apart, with the most typical schedule being at 8 weeks, 12, and finally 16. The DA2PP vaccine should be boostered at age one for maximum efficacy. Many veterinarians claim this series of shots is effective for three years; however, much evidence supports that vaccinating again so soon is unnecessary and poses health risks for your puppy. As an alternative, speak to your veterinarian about a routine blood test called a titer. Titering tests for remaining antibodies in your dog's body from its initial set of core vaccines. Should sufficient antibodies linger in your dog's system, it is unnecessary to vaccinate the dog again.

Your dog should also receive a Rabies shot at six months of age or later if possible. Though many veterinarians do recommend boostering the Rabies shot at one year of age, leading vaccination experts say this is unnecessary. If you are uncertain about what is best for your Cavapoo, you can always schedule an appointment to discuss proper vaccination options with your veterinarian.

## Should You Give Your Cavapoo Vitamins?

Though vitamins do support the proper health and development of your Cavapoo, your dog should receive everything they need via their food. This is where choosing a high-quality diet is so important. If your dog is lacking in vitamins, your veterinarian will make note of it and can recommend the best means to supplement your dog for optimal health. It is never advised that you supplement your Cavapoo's vitamin intake without direct instructions from your veterinarian.

## Keeping Your Cavapoo at a Healthy Weight

It is very important to your Cavapoo's overall health that you keep its weight in check. To do this, you will want to strike the right balance between how much activity your dog gets on a daily basis and how much food it receives.

In general, excess weight is not an issue for the Cavapoo so long as you are committed to taking your dog for a daily walk and pre-measuring your dog's food to ensure correct amounts. A combination of the right amount of exercise with the correct amount of food is key to your dog's success when it comes to a healthy weight.

Poor quality foods that are full of filler ingredients can add an extra layer of padding to your dog's frame pretty quickly. This is undesirable as it can cause undue strain on the sensitive skeletal and muscular systems, causing pain and injury.

The amount of food you feed is also very important. Free feeding should always be discouraged because your dog will surely gobble up far too much if given the opportunity! However, the amount of food you feed is directly proportionate to what you feed. Some foods which are higher in protein content will fill your Cavapoo much quicker. As a result, you can feed much less of this food and still maintain a healthy weight and excellent body condition. For more precise measurements, read the label of the food you feed and follow the guidelines given for your dog's specific weight and size. If your dog is very active, you may need to give an additional amount to satisfy your pooch's hunger. However, always increase amounts only incrementally to prevent weight gain.

## What is the Cavapoo Growth Chart?

As a cross-breed, the Cavapoo currently has no specific growth chart of its own. However, we can use this standard chart of common growths for medium-sized breeds as a benchmark for the Cavapoo.

Here is a general guideline of what you can expect for your Cavapoo puppy (multiply x 2.2 to find your dog's weight in pounds):

### Growth Chart for Medium-Sized Breeds

| Age | Weight |
| --- | --- |
| 8 weeks | 1.6-3.6 kg |
| 4 months | 3.6-7.2 kg |
| 6 months | 5.8-11.7 kg |
| 8 months | 7.9-15.8 kg |
| 10 months | 9.7-19.5 kg |
| 12 months | 11.7-23.5 kg |

## What is a Healthy Amount of Food for a Cavapoo?

Experts recommend feeding your Cavapoo between 1 cup to 1 ½ cups of food per day.

You can adjust the amount of food your dog receives based on the amount of activity you do on a daily basis. Always bear in mind that training treats do add up quickly so you will need to reduce the size of your Cavapoo's meals if you are doing a lot of training.

# CHAPTER 13

# Cavapoos—The Golden Years

Unfortunately, our beloved Cavapoos will get old. Your aging Cavapoo deserves the best of care, and you are only too happy to provide it. The first thing you will notice in a geriatric Cavapoo is slowing down. This is often the first indication that your dog may be experiencing some pain as a result of arthritis. Old age often means adjusting activity lengths for the Cavapoo. Your dog will have the spirit to take on adventures, but the flesh is often too weak to tackle the distances and durations of old. But that's okay! Lots of good times still await you. You'll just need to change your activities to things your dog can still enjoy and not suffer for later. With excellent care, your Cavapoo can still enjoy having fun with you!

## Cavapoo Changes in the Golden Years

Each dog is different, so determining which year begins the golden years for your Cavapoo is hard to predict. As a general guideline, veterinarians consider eight to be the year a dog becomes a senior. Once your dog reaches this magic number, you may start to see a number of changes that you should take note of.

## *Cavapoo Physiological Changes*

Cavapoos will undergo many of the same changes that humans experience as they age. Some of the things to be on the lookout for are arthritis, hearing loss, stiff joints, reduced bladder capacity, and pain.

## *Cavapoo Behavioral Changes*

Your Cavapoo may exhibit some behavioral changes. Most of these can be attributed to senses that are no longer as sharp as they once were. Your Cavapoo's eyes and ears may not work as well as they once did. Even your dog's memory may not be as acute as it was during its younger years. Older Cavapoos startle much more easily, and though it is hard to believe, you may even see some signs of crankiness. This personality change is often the result of aching joints and bones.

# Cavapoo Health—Caring for Your Geriatric Cavapoo

Caring for an aging Cavapoo requires a different approach. Here are some things you should do to help your Cavapoo remain comfortable during the geriatric years:

* **Make regular visits to your veterinarian**

  Regular wellness checks are crucial to staying on top of your Cavapoo's overall health. For best results, visit your veterinarian every six months. This will allow your vet the opportunity to make a note of any changes in your dog, which could be indicative of larger problems. This is key to helping your senior dog remain mobile and happy.

- Avoid rough play

  Your Cavapoo might be getting up there in years, but in its mind, it is still just a young pup that loves to party! This is where you must step in to protect your dog from itself. Your geriatric Cavapoo might think it is still up roughhousing with the young punks only to suffer the consequences at a later date. To keep your dog from suffering an injury, limit playtime to shorter durations and supervise well to prevent any activity that might lead to pain or injury. If you have young, exuberant dogs in the house or puppies, it may be best to restrict their access to your older dog.

- **Limit exercise**

  Your Cavapoo might still think it can tackle the New York Marathon, but you know better. Adjust your dog's walking routine to reasonable amounts that accurately reflect your dog's age and physical condition. When it comes to activity for an old dog, moderation is key.

- **Change to a senior-friendly food**

  Since your Cavapoo will experience a reduction in activity in its senior years, it will no longer require a higher caloric food. Now is the time to switch to a senior formulation that is lower in protein and calories. This will help prevent weight gain as well as provide support for your dog's kidney and liver. As with younger Cavapoos, you will still want to purchase the best quality food that you can afford.

- **Provide access to clean drinking water**

  Some Cavapoos experience reduced kidney function in their senior years. Promote optimal health by ensuring your dog has lots of access to clean drinking water at all times. Dehydration is the enemy of good health.

- **Consider warmth**

  Your elderly Cavapoo could more easily catch a chill. Now is the time to purchase that heated bed you've had your eye on for a while. You can also make your own heated bed by adding a heating pad to an existing donut style bed. Blankets are always welcomed by seniors, and some dogs also like to wear sweaters to stave off the cold.

- **Provide help with stairs**

  You may find your Cavapoo is no longer able to safely go up and down stairs. If this sounds like your dog, you may need to start carrying your dog up and down stairs when needed.

  If your family spends a lot of time in an area of the house with lots of stairs, it may be time to relocate to an area where your dog can be with you without having to go up and down flights of stairs that could lead to a painful fall.

- **Make the most of your time**

  Sadly, the senior years do mean your dog is entering the final stages of life. Each moment is precious. Make the most of it by lavishing your dog with your time and your affection as much as possible.

## Cavapoo Endings—Saying Goodbye to Your Senior Cavapoo

It is never easy to say goodbye. When your dog no longer seems to find joy in day to day living, it is often time to take that final trip to the veterinarian.

No one can really help you make the decision when it is time for your Cavapoo to move from this earthly realm to something more heavenly. It is not a decision you should take lightly, nor is it one that should be made because of pressure from outside voices. The one person who can provide helpful counsel is your veterinarian, who can provide you with an accurate assessment of your dog's health condition as you ponder what to do for your cherished friend.

There is no question that you will grieve the loss of your Cavapoo. Since grieving is so highly unique, do not pressure yourself to feel one way or another. Allow yourself to experience all of the emotions in your heart. Your process may be very different from someone else's. In a way, that is quite fitting as no other dog owner experienced quite what you did with your most special friend. Be patient with yourself, and take all of the time you need to heal. In time, your memories of your beloved friend will be a balm to your heart. Thankfully, neither the memories nor your precious Cavapoo will ever be forgotten.

# CHAPTER 14

# Conclusion

Is the Cavapoo the dog for you? If you are a person who loves adventure, you won't be disappointed with the addition of a Cavapoo to your home. This sunny, laid back breed is a wonderful family companion whose sweet nature will bring a smile to your face every day. Though a breed that is relatively new to the dog scene, the Cavapoo is one pooch that is here to stay!

*Owning a Cavapoo will change your life...for the better.*

The Cavapoo is a breed that can serve many purposes. From scent detection to obedience skills to retrieval work or just being a couch potato, this versatile breed does it all! Today, the Cavapoo is most often found as a beloved family companion.

If you think a Cavapoo may be the dog for you, be sure to do your research and save yourself a lot of heartache by only buying a dog from a reputable breeder. Take care to stay far away from puppy mills and large commercial breeding operations. Be very wary about online marketplaces which can also lead you astray. You will recognize a reputable breeder by their commitment to strict health testing as well as written health guarantee, showing their willingness to provide support for the life of your puppy. By knowing ahead of time what questions you should ask your potential breeder, you will be able to easily determine if the person is someone whose word and ethics you can trust.

Cavapoos have excellent longevity and are a breed with few health concerns. The main things you will need to be aware of include hips, elbows, eyes, patellas, thyroid, and heart problems. Always ask to see health clearances of the parents of your puppy to set your mind at ease that they are free of genetic markers, which could indicate the presence of these issues in your breeder's lines, and thus, your puppy.

Owning and caring for a Cavapoo will not cost you any more money than you would pay for any other breed. However, you will still need to be committed to providing the best quality food that you can afford and regular veterinary care. You will also need to provide your dog with lots of toys and exercise to keep your dog physically and mentally stimulated each day.

Perhaps the most important thing of all is being certain that you are prepared to commit yourself to the care and raising of a Cavapoo. There are additional responsibilities attached to dog ownership, and you must have the time and willingness to commit to ensuring your Cavapoo remains a healthy and well-adjusted family pet. A thorough understanding of the breed will help you find the ideal pooch for your family. You will be glad you spent the time and effort to find the ideal Cavapoo for your home. Once you get your first Cavapoo, you'll be hooked! The breed is so lovable that they are hard to resist. Enjoy your journey as a proud owner of a beautiful Cavapoo!

# Your Comprehensive Cavapoo Resource List

## Cavapoo Breeders in the USA

- **Foxglove Farm**

  https://www.foxglovecavachonpuppies.com/about-cavapoos

  Located in the Midwestern United States

  Foxglove Farm Cavapoos pride themselves on producing healthy, well-socialized puppies from health-tested parents.

- **Pinewood Cavapoos**

  https://pinewoodcavapoos.com/

  Located in the United States (email breeder for the precise location)

  Pinewood Cavapoos specializes in producing healthy companion dogs.

- **Golden Valley Puppies**

  https://goldenvalleypuppies.com/

  Located in Mississippi

  Golden Valley Puppies prides themselves on providing well-socialized Cavapoo puppies for family companionship.

- **Hill Peak Pups**

  http://www.hillpeakpups.com/cavapoos/

  Located in the United States (email breeder for precise location)

  Hill Peak Pups produces Cavapoo puppies of exceptional temperaments from health- tested parents.

- **Recherche Cavs**

  https://trainedcavs.com/

  Located in the United States (email breeder for precise location)

  Recherche Cavs is committed to proper health testing practices to ensure healthy puppies.

- **Whistle Hill Puppies**

  https://www.whistlehillpuppies.com/puppies-for-sale

  Located In the United States (email the breeder for precise location)

  Whistle Hill Puppies prides themselves on producing companion Cavapoos who excel as family pets.

- **Calla Lily Cavapoos**

  **http://www.callalilycavapoo.com/**

  Located in the United States (email breeder for precise location)

  Calla Lily Cavapoos place a high priority on producing puppies from health-tested parents of sound temperament.

- **Ayers Pampered Pets**

  **https://www.ayerspamperedpets.net/**

  Located in Georgia

  Ayers Pampered Pets proudly produces healthy puppies who make ideal family companions. Their dogs have won awards internationally.

- **Cavapoos R Us**

  **http://cavapoosrus.com/**

  Located in the United States (email breeder for precise location)

  Cavapoos R Us takes pride in producing health-tested and well-socialized puppies from champion bloodlines.

- **Petit Jean Puppies**

  **https://www.petitjeanpuppies.com/**

  Located in Arkansas

  Petit Jean Puppies is a high-quality breeder of Cavapoos in existence from 1998.

- **Crockett Doodles**

  **https://www.crockettdoodles.com/cavapoos**

  Located in the United States (email breeder for precise location)

  Crockett Doodles is a breeder of Cavapoos backed by solid peer reviews. They have a reputation for producing outstanding dogs.

- **Absolutely Elegant Kennels**
  **http://www.aekennels.com/**
  Located in Georgia
  Absolutely Elegant Kennels is a veterinarian run kennel operation specializing in healthy, temperamentally sound Cavapoos.

- **Darling Doodles and Poos**
  **https://www.darlingdoodlesandpoos.com/**
  **Located in Minneapolis**
  Darling Doodles and Poos is a small hobby kennel focusing on providing happy, healthy Cavapoo puppies for family homes.

- **Mulberry Farm**
  **http://www.mulberryfarm.com/**
  Located in New York
  Mulberry Farm is a Doodle and Cavapoo breeder located on a farm in New York state.

- **Howdee Kennels**
  **https://www.howdeekennel.com/**
  Located in Washington
  A small home-based kennel specializing in Cavapoos

- **Cedar Rose Kennels**

  **http://www.cedarrosekennels.com/cavapoos**

  Located in Georgia

  Cedar Rose Kennels focuses on producing on small, high-quality litters of Cavapoos.

- **Designer Dogs of America**

  **https://www.designerdogsofamerica.com/breeders**

  Designer Dogs of America is a comprehensive list of Cavapoo breeders in the USA.

## Cavapoo Breeders in Canada

- **Pleasant Meadow Cavapoos**

  https://www.pleasantmeadowscanada.com/

  Located in Ontario

  Pleasant Meadows Cavapoos places a high emphasis on producing well-socialized puppies of excellent health and temperament.

- **Country Home Kennels**

  https://www.chkennels.net/information

  Located in Canada (email breeder for precise location)

  Country Home Kennels is a breeder of several different "Doodle" types. Their Cavapoos are backed by a health guarantee.

- **Stoney Acre Puppies**

  https://stoneyacrepuppies.weebly.com/

  Located in Ontario

  Stoney Acre Puppies is a small breeding operation with only a handful of litters per year. Their puppies are from health-tested parents of excellent conformation and temperament.

- **Three Shades Cavapoos**

  **https://www.ranchsantagato.com/cavapoos**

  Located in Canada (email breeder for precise location)

  Three Shades Cavapoos offers high quality, well-socialized Cavapoo puppies available several times per year.

- **A&R Country Kennel**

  **http://www.arcountrykennel.com/**

  Located in Ontario

  A&R Country Kennel takes pride in producing Cavapoo puppies of sound temperament.

- **Cavapoos of Ontario**

  **https://cavapoosofontario.com/**

  Located in Ontario

  Cavapoos of Ontario is a small hobby kennel with a focus on providing health-tested, stable puppies for families to enjoy.

## Cavapoo Breeders in Australia

- **Diamond Valley Kennels**

  **https://dvkennels.com.au/about/**

  Located in Queensland

  Diamond Kennels offers boarding services and has a few Cavapoo puppy litters each year.

- **Pocket Puppies**

  **https://www.pocketpuppies.com.au/**

  Located near Sydney

  Pocket Puppies specializes in Toy Cavapoos.

- **Chevromist Kennels**

  **https://www.chevromist.com/cavoodles/**

  Located in Australia (email breeder for precise location)

  Chevromist Kennels offers healthy Cavapoo puppies well-suited to family homes.

- **Billabong Creek Farm**

  **https://www.billabongcreekfarm.com.au/**

  Located in Victoria

  Billabong Creek Farm is committed to breeding from health-tested parent stock.

- **Cottage Canines**
  **http://www.cottagecanines.com/cavoodles.html**
  Located in Sydney
  Cottage Canines are registered breeders who occasionally have puppies available to approved homes.

## Cavapoo Breeders in the UK

- **Henley Cavapoos and Maltipoos**
  **http://www.henleypoos.co.uk/home/**
  Located in the UK (email breeder for precise location)
  A small breeding kennel with focus on producing healthy puppies

- **Raffles Cockapoos**
  **https://www.rafflescockapoos.co.uk/cavapoo-2**
  Located in the UK (email breeder for the precise location)
  A kennel focusing on the breeding of healthy designer dogs. Cavapoo puppies are available occasionally to approved families.

- **Posh Poos**
  **https://poshpoos.co.uk/**
  Located in Surrey
  Posh Poos breeds designer dogs including Cavapoos.

- Chamuel Puppies

  **https://www.chamuelpuppies.co.uk/**

  Located in Essex

  Registered breeders of Cavapoos

- Lorton Cockapoos

  **http://www.lortoncockapoos.co.uk/**

  Located in the UK (email breeder for precise location)

  Registered breeder of designer dog breeds including the Cavapoo

## Cavapoo Rescue Shelters in the USA

- Poo-Mix Rescue

  **https://poomixrescue.com/**

  Online resource

  Poo-Mix Rescue is an online resource where people can list Cavapoos and other mixes available for adoption. Their main focus is cross-breeds and hybrids.

## Cavapoo Rescue Shelters in the UK

- **The Doodle Trust**

  https://www.doodletrust.com/

  The only rescue shelter in the UK dealing primarily with cross-breeds, The Doodle Trust places emphasis on finding homes for unwanted Doodles in need of new homes.

## Cavapoo Registration Services and Breeder Resources in the USA and UK

- **International Designer Canine Registry (IDCR)**

  http://designercanineregistry.com

  The International Designer Canine Registry offers registration services and pedigree tracking for designer dog breeds. They are also a resource for sourcing breeders of Cavapoos in your region.

- **National Hybrid Registry (NHR)**

  http://www.nationalhybridregistry.com

  The National Hybrid Registry is a registering body for designer dogs.

- **Designer Dogs—The Kennel Club**

  https://www.thekennelclub.org.uk/our-resources/media-centre/issue-statements/designer-dogs/

  A UK-based registration service, Designer Dogs-The Kennel Club is a registering organization and a resource that seeks to unite dog seekers with dog breeders.

Made in the USA
Coppell, TX
30 May 2020

26676296R00089